SKELLIGSIDE
Southern Iveragh

IRELAND

•Belfast
•Sligo
•Galway Dublin•
•Limerick
•Tralee •Cork

Puff
Is

ATLANTIC OCEAN

Lemon
Rock

Little
Skellig

Great
Skellig

N

0 1 2 3 4

MILES

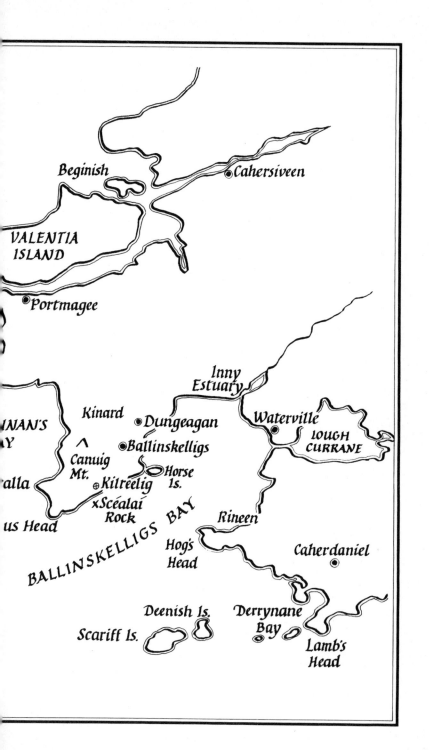

Skelligside

for Nancy and Max

Skelligside

Michael Kirby

THE LILLIPUT PRESS

First published in 1990 by
THE LILLIPUT PRESS LTD
4 Rosemount Terrace, Arbour Hill,
Dublin 7, Ireland

A CIP record for this
title is available from
The British Library.

ISBN 0 946640 52 1
ISBN 0 946640 53 X pbk

Jacket design by Jole Bortoli
Set in 11.5 on 13 Garamond by
Seton Music Graphics Ltd of Bantry
and printed in Dublin by
Colour Books of Baldoyle

Contents

PREFACE

Whether by desire, design, or accident on the part of my good parents, I squawked and squalled my way in 1906 into the Gaeltacht of Ballinskelligs on the southern shore of the beautiful Iveragh peninsula. Sleeping and crying as a child, laughing and talking as a boy, the constant music of the Gaelic tongue fell softly on my ear. The language of the *Sasanach* was seldom used in our family or among the neighbours.

At national school I experienced a new set of growing pains, pains of a physical as well as a mental nature. The master was a stickler for accuracy, and when English was in session he would growl and wield his hazel wand, shouting 'Watch your grammar!' I learned English not through curiosity or love, but in fear and trembling.

I have tried to write with honesty and from the heart, presenting to the reader a picture in story of rural life in Ballinskelligs during the first half of the twentieth century. Many of the little things which fitted into the jigsaw of our daily lives have now, alas, become only a memory. Therefore I give you *Skelligside*, a glimpse into the simple life once lived by our ancestors.

Michael Kirby

I
My Own Place

AN EARLY SCHOOLING

My mother, Mary Cremin, told me that no professional medical aid was available on the night I was born. A local woman, who knew the traditional skills of midwifery given to her from generations, gently directed and delivered me over the threshold of the womb into this world. I drew my first breath on 31 May 1906. I was the last of the little clutch of five boys and two girls.

At the age of five I was sent to school. I remember being neatly dressed in a skirt of blue frieze, and a frilled pinafore tied with white tape across my back. Few wore boots and trousers in my class. The master, Cornelius Shanahan, entered my name in the school roll and kindly presented me with a penny. But alas, on that same day I came to grief. While playing in the school yard I fell across a shallow pool and lost that first penny. My sister Sheila took my hand in hers and led me home with soothing words. Thus ended my first day at school.

As time went by I got used to school routine, though I was not in love with learning yet. The master's snake-like hazel rod was eternally busy. Because of my slow rate of progress in arithmetic, the portion of my anatomy between rib-cage and buttocks was massaged by that same rod. I would rather see the devil himself than the long tot on the blackboard: I often reached the top figure helped by several applications of hazel.

Everything about my schooldays now seems to belong to the Stone Age, even the blue-black slates we used instead of copybooks, with pencils of the same material. Pupils had to stand back-to-back in twos to prevent copying, though we would sometimes whisper words or figures to each other when the teacher was not looking.

The grown boys played football in the little field attached to the school. The ball was made of long cloth strips, wound solidly and hand-sewn with every conceivable kind of twine. It had a certain amount of dull bounce, and it made do. Many boys wore long flannel skirts, often pleated like the Scottish kilt. Sometimes it was impossible to differentiate between the sexes, except when the boys held up their skirts to water the lawn.

During play-hour a team was picked of ten a side. The game waxed fast and furious, no quarter given and no quarter called for, no referee, no set rules, the pupils on the sideline urging on their favourites. After the game it was not unusual to notice some of the warriors nursing minor injuries: maybe a bloody nose, or a pendant of flesh hanging from a bare foot, where a big toe had been stubbed against a jutting ground-stone. Our teacher, a kind-hearted man who missed no opportunity to perform a good deed, would immediately apply some ointments he kept stored in a cupboard for such emergencies.

Many and varied were the games played in my young days. We played games with stones, such as casting a stone from the shoulder. The cast was made from a special mark. The weight of the stone varied – light, medium or heavy, three pounds, six pounds, or eight pounds. It was usually round, clumsy, smooth and difficult to grasp. The throw had to come straight from the shoulder, and any step over the line meant disqualification for the contender. It is said that nimbleness beats strength, so a brawny contestant was sometimes defeated by a lean and scrawny opponent, much to the delight of the onlookers. I remember rounders being played when we were schoolchildren. I do not recall the rules, except that it was not unlike cricket. Several players stood in the formation of a wide ring using a crude round bat or stick. After a strike a series of runs took place before the ball was retrieved. The ball consisted of sewn leather filled with some substance like sawdust.

Another game called 'ducks off' was extremely dangerous to both spectators and participants. The ducks were pieces of round hard stone three or four pounds in weight. A large flat stone was placed about fifty feet from the line where each throw was made. This stone was called the 'Granny'. The ducks were first rolled from the line towards the flat table by a team of six boys. The boy whose duck was found to be farthest away from the 'Granny' was obliged to place it on the table to be shot at by the other boys. After each throw, a scramble would ensue for the boys to get back to the line if the stone remained stationary on the table: those who failed to get back to line on time would be eliminated. This game was intricate, and dangerous to participate in. One of our players suffered a blow to the head which made him temporarily unconscious. Before collapsing, he put his hand to his head and exclaimed 'Oh boys, I am dead forever!'

The teacher warned us not to loiter on our way home after school. We were fond of delaying near an old ruined house by the roadside, where we played various harmless games such as long leap, hop step and jump, and frog's leap. One particular contest led to our undoing. This was a competition to find the boy who could piss the highest. It meant pissing over the wall of the old ruin which had different levels and was ideally suited for the purpose.

Some busybody who had seen the boys at play told the teacher of our pranks, and he punished us and informed our parents. My mother was appalled. She exhorted me to change my evil ways and to confess my sins immediately. I lived in terrible fear of God, though to me He seemed a much nicer person than the teacher or the priest. We did not consider our competition to be so sinful or obscene. It was great fun while the water lasted. I do not know if any records were broken. One boy pissed sideways, so because of his poor aim he was barred from the contest. It was not considered safe to stand near him while competing. We called him Paddy Sideways. Later on we were bombarded with hell-fire, brimstone and eternal damnation. We were labelled as young blackguards by the breast-thumping holy-water hens who were usually whispering into the ear of the village pump. They foretold we would eventually bring ruin and shame on our respectable parents.

For me there was a second fall from grace during that school year. I was coming nine years old. My mother kept a flock of Rhode Island Red hens, and with them a beautiful strutting rooster. The creature had a curved tail like a golden rainbow with a few blue-green feathers for decoration, two bright looping gills hung like rubies from his jowl, and his slender yellow legs were adorned with formidable spurs. I think he was my mother's 'sacred cow'. He would perform a pirouette in front of her when she fed the hens.

One evening as I arrived home from school he was standing supreme on the doorstep of our kitchen. I tried to walk past but he attacked me by flying in my face. I aimed a kick at him and blurted out, 'Be off, or I'll kick your bloody arse!' My mother nearly fainted upon hearing my new language. She took me inside and started to wig my ears. My father, who was weaving a lobster pot, intervened. 'Don't be harsh,' he said, 'he is only learning.' Looking back now, we were a group of young mischievous scally-wags who were wont to break the standards of behaviour required by the strict rules of the time.

Ballinskelligs National School was built in the year 1867. A hedge school catered for the locality until then. On the first day of July 1909, the school was allowed bilingual status. The region was densely populated before the Great War of 1914, and all the people spoke the melodious and subtle Irish of the region. English Schools' Inspectors conducted all examinations in those years – Dale, Welpley, Lehane, Alexander and Cussen. I often saw the teacher grow pale on their arrival in the classroom – he would not expect an iota of pity from these grim-faced taskmasters.

Examinations on Religious Instruction took place once a year. The inspector was usually a Catholic priest who often conducted the examination in English. Some of the senior boys were show-ing poetic talent by composing light religious poetry:

'Who made the world?'
'Paddy Fitzgerald
With a spade
and a shovel.'

The infant class were not slow at learning from their elders, so the Reverend Examiner was astonished to hear from the smaller children that Paddy Fitzgerald was a powerful deity, much to the consternation of the teacher, who seemed to suffer hot flushes. I remember one question put to a pupil in my class: 'Did God create the devil, my child?' The answer came in faltering English:

'He warn't any devil when He made him, Father.' Another question: 'When were you born, my child?' brought the reply: 'The night of the Biddy, Father!' The child meant she was born on the feast of St Brigid. Nevertheless, we had a good grasp of the catechism and all aspects of the faith, and the priest usually gave us good marks.

Neither priest nor monk, father nor mother, nor even the teacher himself told us anything about the birds and the bees. It was not right for us to mention sexual matters. I did not know exactly where I came from. Now, when my body was growing and my sexual organs were awakening, I thought something very strange was happening to me.

I understood from the faint whisperings that sex was very sinful – sinful to speak of, to think of, to look at, to touch, to read about or listen to. That very same sex was swallowing souls into hell every moment. An old man I questioned about it said 'Blind people are a great pity.' Everything about sex was a mysterious secret in my youthful days. Those who fell victim then to the pleasures of the flesh caused a public scandal.

I remember the first time I laid my eyes on a naked young woman. She was having a swim nearby one summer's day. Every vein in my body burst into flame. Beauty drew me to her, a beauty kept secret from me until then. Then a sudden fear possessed me. Is this original sin, the seed of all sin? Is it Satan who creates this desire in me – a deadly mortal sin in front of me? Oh, blind people are a great pity! So the old man said.

THE RICHES OF THE SEA

When I had grown a little older and my bones were stretching, the Great War broke out. What a change it brought into being! The old adage says that Death is seen on the face of the old man and on the back of the youth. Destruction and shipwreck were visited on the south coast during that time. Sudden death lurked beneath those once peaceful waters, now a hiding-place for powerful submarines of the warring nations. Many a proud merchant ship was sent without warning to the bottom of the sea – the crew unable to take to the boats before the deafening roar of the exploding torpedo. Within minutes nothing was left but little pieces of torn wood and the corpse of a sailor being borne away on the ocean stream.

All kinds of wreckage came ashore on Ballinskelligs beaches then, including empty lifeboats and dead bodies from the *Lusitania*. A substantial reward was offered to the person who discovered the body of Mr Vanderbilt, the American banker and millionaire who perished in the sinking of that great ship. Police and coast-watchers scoured the beaches of Cork, Kerry and Clare in search of his remains. It was rumoured that these were found on the Clare coast in an advanced stage of decomposition.

On New Year's Eve 1916 four hundred wooden casks of white paraffin came ashore at the little beach in the creek of Boolakeel. The entire population of the little hamlet converged on the beach and rolled the casks to a place of safety above the breakers. Some took barrels home, but to no avail. Members of the Royal Irish Constabulary came and searched every house, every field and dyke, even the manure heaps. My neighbour had a few gallons stored in a tub in the cowhouse, where they were found by the sergeant. He took the tub to the doorway and spilled its contents into the drain. I do not wonder why the people rebelled against British rule in Ireland.

Fish was plentiful during those years. My father bought a small rowing boat, specially ordered to his own dimensions, for line and lobster fishing. The first I took on board myself was a pollack about eight pounds in weight, but I imagined it was as big as a horse. My father praised me on how well I handled it. I was eight years old then. By the age of ten, with constant practice, I had mastered the art of rowing with short paddles. We filled large casks with white fish, mostly pollack and cod, cured in brine and dried, and my father sold it for three pence per pound. Many a day we would row westward under the great cliffs of Bolus to the most likely places, which my father would pinpoint by getting certain landmarks on shore into line. When he reached the desired position he would order me to cast the mooring-stone and make fast. As soon as we had our hooks baited with glistening cubes of fresh mackerel or mussel and set for bottom fishing, we were kept busy hauling until the little boat was heavy with a varied catch of codling, red sea bream, large whiting, grey and red gurnard, ling and ray. Those were halcyon days of my youth, which time will never erode from the living cells of my memory.

One day while we were westward in the bay, my father took what seemed to be a heavy fish on his line. After a long struggle, he caught sight of the great creature for a fleeting moment. He knew immediately it was a large halibut. No sooner had the fish surfaced than it plunged again to the depths of the sea, taking all of thirty-five fathoms of line singing over the gunwale in its wake. My father paid out line when necessary, and also took up the slack. At one time the fish leaped clear out of the water and fell over on its back, sending a shower of white spray heavenward. But it failed to dislodge the small whiting hook stuck firmly in its jaw muscle. This exciting struggle continued for some time, with the fish slicing the water like a broad spear. It was lovely to watch the seasoned old fisherman deftly handling the pressure on the line. Only one golden rule had to be followed: not to let the fish break you when your gear was too light for the burden. After some time my father spoke urgently to me: 'Get the gaff and look out for him!' I knew then that the great tussle was nearly over. The noble heart of the fish had weakened, and its pulse was a mere fluttering. My father eased it gently toward the side of the boat into my reach, and I sank the barb of the gaff deeply in its side. I helped my father take the fish on board. '*Ó, a Mhuire!*' exclaimed my father, 'Oh, Virgin, what a beautiful fish!' It was a little short of ninety pounds, and it took only a small whiting hook and a cube of fresh mackerel to do the job.

I often listened to the old people tell of the Great Famine and how many of Ireland's poor fled to the coast for survival. A million people are thought to have died in Munster during the Famine period. Thousands came to the rocky beaches and sandy inlets searching for shellfish – limpets, winkles, mussels, cockles, crabs, sand eels and rockling. Edible seaweed – sea dulse, *miabhán,* carrageen, green *sleaidí* – was boiled and eaten. Ballan wrasse and gunnar wrasse were very plentiful. People were seen to fish from every vantage point, even on the rocks of the most dangerous headlands. All that was needed were some small hooks, a piece of line made from home-grown flax, some lugworms for bait and a stone for a sinker. This crude fishing tackle could mean the difference between survival and death. Large hake were plentiful in the inshore waters of the south and west coast. The trawl had not yet been invented and the large foreign steam trawlers did not arrive for many a year to come. Local fishermen also brought gannets from the Great Skellig, which they salted and used as food. I heard of how the English agent who collected the land rent saw many large fish in my grandfather's house. He warned that the rent would be increased if the landlord became aware of how well off we were.

Because of fishing, the death rate from hunger was not so high on the coast. One old woman, called the Fishing Hag, was well known in the area during the Famine. Many tales were told about her powers of attracting fish wherever she cast a hook. She always kept a supply of salted fish strapped to her back to prevent it being stolen, as hordes of people roamed the roads of Munster in quest of food. This poor old woman did not have a name and never told anyone who she was. The Fishing Hag died in the house where I was born. The neighbours and my people made her coffin, and as night was falling it was brought across the fields and buried in the old graveyard by the sea that was once St Michael's Abbey. It was by the light of bogdeal torches that the last sod was laid on her grave.

There was a place near the old graveyard which was called Bearna na gCorp or the Gap of the Corpses. So many people died each day during the Famine that it was impossible to bury them all, and some were left near the opening in the wall until the next day.

*   *   *

'Today is Rabharta Rua na hInide, the Red Tide of Lent,' said my father. 'Carraig an Eascú will be exposed, so bring the long holly rod from the rafters of the cow byre.'

'But, Dad,' I said, 'the holly rod has neither line nor sinker this many a long day.'

'That makes no difference, son. On certain days, you can get fish with a rod without a line or sinker.'

I did as I was bidden. I took the seasoned holly rod from the rafters and brought it along. It was all of eight feet in length and tapered to a point. 'I'll bring the gaff, a sack, and my knife too,' said Dad. 'There's an old saying: a fisherman without a knife, a greyhound without a tail, a ship without a rudder. Come! Let's go. You never know where lurks a lobster.'

My young heart fluttered with wings of joy as I went to search the exposed harbour reefs with a master fisherman. Standing on the shingle beach which overlooked the strand, we could see that the Rinn Dubh, the Black Reef, was entirely exposed, the Lough of the Dulce without a drop of ocean.

The sweet edible sea dulce lay in great fallen swathes like a field of ripe corn after heavy rain, losing some of its iodine content in the bleaching of the noonday sun. Because I was barefoot, Dad told me to be careful when wading in the pools lest I tread on a sea urchin. It was my first time seeing the marine anemones with their beautiful coloured fringes. I thought it odd to see things like cows' teats growing on rounded boulders beneath the sea. I questioned Dad about what form of life they were, so very strange did they appear to me. 'Nothing new, my boy! nothing new,' he replied. 'Scientists call them *Metredium Dianthus* . Take to the books, boy, take to the books.' Ah! but Dad was droll.

The colours of the different anemones fascinated me. Some were ruby, some were pink and blood-red, others a mixture of green and greyish blue, their delicate feathery fringes forever opening and closing, capturing the plankton they relied on for their existence. Dad explained that many microscopic forms of life exist on both land and sea whose time has not yet arrived to be of benefit to mankind. Years later, I read some more about lesser forms of life, but I have come to the conclusion that my greatest problem is trying to understand myself.

My father showed me a narrow gravel bed between the rocks, where the cockles are found. Burrowing beneath the loose gravel, he found smooth and tiger-tooth cockles, and very soon I was able to find them on my own. We put a quantity of the choicest ones in the bag. 'It is not so much in quest of cockles that we're here,' said my father, 'so give me the holly rod, and we'll search for lobster. Perhaps it's yet early, after winter, but an old "Jack" may be hibernating.'

My father started to search, thoroughly and methodically, all the flat slabs of rock in the pools. He poked the slender end of the rod underneath, and explained to me what signs to look for. 'The lobster is a hermit by nature,' said he, 'and will stay under a flat rock or boulder for long periods. He has usually two doors to his dwelling, an entrance and an exit. If the rock is on sand or gravel bottom, the front door will be like a rabbit burrow.'

I noticed a rock in the middle of a pool, which had about twelve inches of water around it, and because I did not have boots, Dad gave me the rod, telling me to poke underneath in the place which he indicated. When I inserted that rod I felt as if something caught hold of its tip. 'He's in there,' said Dad, 'Deal roughly with him: push the rod quickly!' No sooner said than done: the lobster came rushing out tail first, making a clapping noise through the shallow water. I was about to grasp it, but it reached both its claws upwards menacingly. 'I'll show you how to lift a lobster,' said the master. 'Slip your open hand under his armpits from the back, and grasp it firmly; a lobster can inflict serious wounds, especially with the scissors claw.'

My father reached into the water and lifted out a nice two-pound lobster. He then sat on a rock, placed the lobster between his knees, and deftly cut the nerves of both claws with his knife, before putting him into a bag which we had for lobsters only. We found two more at the western corner of Rinn Dubh before arriving at the reef underneath the old monastery. The large boulder called Carraig an Eascú lay naked. As we approached it my father said, 'This rock was never without a tenant underneath,' and how right he was! He inserted the steel gaff, and hooked a large black conger eel, which he released onto the strand nearby. I watched it squirm and writhe its way snake-like towards the water after receiving only a minor wound from the gaff.

The Eel Rock yielded only two large, red edible crabs, which my father put on a string. John Shea's house stood near the beach, so Dad asked him for the loan of his spade to dig for green-shelled razor clams, which were to be had in abundance. He dug many hundreds of them, some as thick as thole-pins. When mixed with great oval clams, these make a mouth-watering chowder. The rock pools teemed with marine life: red rockling, speckled blennys and many shrimps could be seen sheltering under the fronds of the sea kelp; rowing crabs, velvet-backs, and green soft crabs swam about in all directions. There were purple sea urchins, whose internal segments are nice to eat. I saw several blue and yellow flat-headed dragonettes in the pools. I have found them in very deep water also. The fish is not edible and their spines can be very poisonous. The sea-mouse and the little scorpion crabs were to be found beneath the sand, when we dug for the clams. Dad showed me where to find rock oysters, the flat shell cemented solidly to the smooth rock, which is always horizontal. The interior has a green-blue, mother-of-pearl glaze, and the top shell takes on the same colour as the background on which it grows, making it difficult to detect. Rock oysters have no food value. Sea cucumbers are found within the ponds and in the dense kelp as well, some brownish-black, soft and boneless, with many hundred sucking discs. Being blind, they have a compensatory sensory intelligence, and exude a white thread-like membrane as a defence. The great spider crab, with its long crooked claws and pear-shaped body, I was introduced to for the first time at the edge of low water, although I became more familiar with its free-loading habits inside my lobster pots in later life.

Queen escallops are found within the harbour on a calm day when shadow is on the water. We used to take them out with a hoop and net mounted on a long pole, and sometimes with a pitchfork. Their flesh is delicious, the orange part having a very savoury taste. Horse whelks were in plentiful supply, but only the black winkle had a commercial value. Yellow winkles, pearl win-kles, striped cone winkles and miniature ear-shells shared pools with hermit crabs, showing one great claw and antenna from with-in an old whelk shell – a curiosity in the vast order of marine life.

The tide had now turned. As we turned our faces homewards I heard Dad murmur to himself, 'The lower the ebb, the sooner the harbour will fill.' I was fortunate in my tutor, who knew his environment so well, though he was hardly aware of the precious gift he was handing down to his son.

*　　*　　*

Lobsters and crayfish were very plentiful, and wherever along the rocky coast you set a pot with good fresh bait you would not look forward in vain to a black haul. The big ones could be found in the deep dark caves which were fished but seldom.

It would depend on the weather being fair and calm to go by rowboat beyond Bolus Head and westward to the cliffs of Dú Chealla. After two or three days' fishing in that area you would return home not empty or poor, but with several dozen lobsters for sale. They were cheap then – five shillings a dozen and often much less. I loved to go west with my father and Michael Curran hauling the pots on moonlit nights. Nothing was more beautiful than to look westward to where the sea and sky met. The planets were like fiery jewels climbing the peaks of heaven, while Dubh Inis and Scariff lay sleeping on the margin of Ballinskelligs Bay. The hills of Iveragh and the great Reeks of Kerry stood in the eastern sky, like giant sentinels guarding the harbours. Over it all the full moon shone, leaving a silver pathway on the waves, as if bright ghosts were dancing on a crystal mirror. You could hear the yawning of seals in their breeding caves. Long wailing cries came to a climax, then slowly died to a last bitter sob. It was like the cry of some lost soul echoing from the dungeons of the damned. On the other hand, it was music to our ears to hear the loud clattering of a lobster when a pot broke the surface, or the rasping of crayfish when they moved their antennae.

Red crab and large marauders of conger eel all went into the pots in pursuit of the free meals put up by the fisherman, and intended for lobsters only. Many different kinds of crab were to be found: the red and green, the rowing crab, the velvet-back, the large spider crabs and the hermit crabs. The fisherman had to deal with all the uninvited guests, replacing all eaten and torn bait before resetting the traps. Unwelcome visitors included the blind sea-leech, the pipefish, the speckled hagfish, the grey nurse, the horned bullhead, the yellow blenny, the pink and purple sea urchin, and the octopus.

Red bream was found in every bay and estuary on the Kerry coast, a delicious fish to eat, with its sweet savoury taste. We had large wooden casks full of pickled bream, which had a ready local market. Far from hunger was the kitchen that could serve potatoes, milk, butter and fresh bream. Whiting and gurnard were also abundant. The red gurnard was called the piper because he has a double air sac resembling bagpipes, while the grey gurnard has only a single one. The old people had great faith in the healing power of gurnard broth, which was good for swollen tonsils and digestive ailments. The broth was very rich, full of a peculiar fat, sweet and invigorating to drink. In my early adolescence I was anxious to find out how I happened into this world. It was unthinkable that I should be told the dire secret that I had come from my mother's womb, so I was fobbed off with the story that my father had found me in the belly of a gurnard. Much as I had liked gurnard broth, I developed a revulsion to it from that time on.

Seine boats were numerous on the south-west coast during my teenage years. Two open boats were used to operate the seine purse net. Each boat was thirty to thirty-five feet long with only a seven-foot beam, and was propelled by six seventeen-foot oars. The seine boat carried the large net and two men operated each oar. The second boat, called the follower, had six single-man oars. This boat took the tow line from the end of the net when it first entered the water, while the other sped swiftly away, casting the net overboard as it encircled the fish school and joined up with the follower. The two boats took eighteen crew members, two skippers and an experienced fisherman who stood upright in the bow. He was the lookout, and director of the haul. His orders were given in a loud clear voice and always in Irish.

Great mackerel and herring schools were to be found in the harvest season, when the phosphorescent light was at its peak during August. The movement of schools of fish in the water looked like light on a dark screen, which was at once detected and appraised by the experienced eye of the lookout navigator. It was he who could tell whether the school was dense or near to the surface, whether it was mackerel or herring or other fish, and what direction and speed it was travelling. The crew would keep the oars out of the water and remain completely silent as he watched his prey from the bow. Some seine boats made good harvest, bringing in large catches of fish night after night. The old castle seine was called Kirby's seine. My father was well versed in the mounting and sewing together of the great purse net, which in order to operate successfully had to be correct in all dimensions. He was sent to Donegal for a term to instruct the fishermen of that area in its use. This instruction was sponsored by the old British Congested Districts' Board.

My father, John Kirby, took the greatest school of fish ever recorded in Ballinskelligs Bay one night in August 1908, west of Bolus Head at a place called Lúb na Leacach or the Loop of the Flagstones. The night was calm, and near the cliff face he saw a small circle of phosphorescence which turned out to be fair and deep. He studied the school for a while and told his crew he intended setting the net between the school and the cliff, as close as possible. When he gave orders for the cliff-face oars to be lifted he wanted no panic, as by then the boat would be at full speed. Now was the time of truth – every man at his sharpest. These are some of the orders you might have heard on that night:

Straighten the boat for me!
Cast net on it!
Take her forward!
All oars together!
Give me speed!
Easy! the net-side oars!
Keep away a little!
Back water the second oar!
Pull hard on the bow oar!
Easy! steady!
Keep coming!

Close the circle. Easy!
Take her forward together!
Give her speed!
More speed!
Back water!
Lift the oars!
Take the holding rope!
Pull us up against the current!

Those last instructions were given to the follower boat, whose job it was to keep the seine boat from drifting into the circle of net while the haul was in progress. This involved hauling the heavy running-rope which ran through a set of metal eye-rings mounted to the bottom of the net. When this was done there was no escape and the purse was considered closed. The work was always carried out through the medium of Irish. It was unheard of for a member of the crew to use English – laughable, like hearing a fart breaking the silence of solemnity. The night that I refer to, the net was set carefully and the great school was trapped. God's blessing seemed to shine on the fishermen of Ballinskelligs. Some of the crew were sent ashore and scaled the cliff face to the roadway above. Their mission was to reach Ballinskelligs, three miles away, to alert the neighbours and bring back as many empty boats as possible. They brought ashore seventy-five thousand prime mackerel that morning, and because of a shortage of empty boats had to release several thousand more. Five seine boats operated from Ballinskelligs harbour, employing more than one hundred fishermen, in those days long gone.

*   *   *

To hear my father say we'd go trammel fishing always filled me with joyful expectation – the joy of a young boy included in men's work. Fishing had a certain call for me.

Michael P. Sugrue of Ballinskelligs West was my father's fishing companion for as long as I can remember. They were both masters of hook, line and sinker, having developed a traditional skill through the practical experience of years. Our fishing boat was carvel-built, twenty-one feet long, and we used it for sea angling, net fishing and lobster pots. We prepared the fishing gear the evening before, carefully boarding the nets into the boat in such a way as to avoid any snagging or entanglement of the meshes when the nets were set into the sea. Trammel nets were mounted to a specially weighted foot-rope, and the top rope was fitted with floats which kept the net standing upright on the bottom of the sea. The nets would be carefully mounted according to a certain formula that served to keep each mesh open in the water (the net could become 'blind' if not properly mounted) and set twenty or more fathoms deep.

It was now nearing the end of August, and time to lay by some casks of cured fish for the winter. The early morning dawned bright and clear. Mike Sugrue, never known to be late, arrived just as the sun was peeping over the Kerry Reeks. My mother waved us goodbye from the door of our cottage and wished us luck with her usual blessing. We quickly walked the few hundred yards to the beach. Mike Sugrue brought the oars which were stored in the castle ruins. I found the bailing bucket and thole-pins which were kept in a hideaway known only to the boatmen. My father had numerous fishing lines coiled on frames ready for use, and several types of fresh bait prepared the day before – fresh mackerel, mussels, lug sandworms and red crab, whose meat is an excellent bait for bottom fishing. Mike Sugrue found a suitable stone to which he attached the long mooring rope for anchoring the little boat in rough or weedy ground. He also attached the heel stones to each net. All ready at last, we pushed the boat into the water, from the pebbly beach in front of the MacCarthy castle. In no time we had our oars in the water and were leaving Carraig on our stern on our way to the Bay Rock, a sunken reef which lies a mile and a half directly east of Horse Island point. There we set the nets carefully.

I was given the task of keeping the boat moving slowly ahead with the short oars. When the nets were set and the buoy lines cast overboard, my father decided we would go westward to a part of the bay known to be a rich ground for bottom fishing. Our boat sped away from each thrust of the oar blades as if eager for angling. We passed by the bealach, known in English as Horse Island Sound, and the cave of Elinore, by Cuas na Móna, the Cave of the Turf. We passed by Boolakeel creek and the Gownach Rock, under the cliffs of Kilreelig, whose whitewashed thatched cottages stood out under the heather-clad hill in the morning sun, the small green paddocks with their dry stone enclosures beautiful to behold. We sped by Carraig an Scéalaí, the Storyteller's Rock. The Cormorants' Cave came into view, and we reached a point where the landmarks my father had in mind came into line. One was the Great Skellig, showing itself just clear of Bolus Head, the other the old fortified observation point on the headland on the shoulder of Canuig Mountain.

My father ordered the boat to be brought to a halt. We stopped rowing, and when the boat had lost all momentum he dropped the mooring-stone overboard with thirty-five fathoms of slack rope. The little craft immediately settled head to wind, which was only a faint breeze from the south-west. The oars were stowed and we all got busy getting the hand-lines ready. My father operated two of these, with different baits, each line having two hooks. Michael Sugrue had already paid out his hand-line baited with mackerel. I was the last to pay out. Being over-anxious to be first, I tangled my line, and my father helped me to unravel it, smiling as he remarked that a peaceful mind helps to undo the tangled skein. Finally I got my line to the bottom. Mike Sugrue said, 'Let's see who will catch the first fish,' and immediately started to haul in two whiting. My father said in Irish, 'Good man! you've broken the spell of the sea witch.' Soon afterwards I felt several faint tugs on my line. I started to haul, and to my surprise brought on board two grey gurnard. When I took them off the hooks they escaped on to the bottom of the boat where they made little croaking noises like frogs in a pond. My father said that the fish were trying to sing but suffered from sore throats because of the wet. Mike Sugrue got busy once more taking on board a very nice codling.

My father was becoming anxious because he was not getting any fish on his lines, and examined his baits carefully. He smelled them in case he had contaminated them with the scent of tobacco from his fingers. Fish are sensitive to smell, and even great sharks are known to swim away from polluted water. Having satisfied himself that all was well, he sent his lines humming over the gunwale once more and soon hauled in several whiting and some white Atlantic pollack. For my part, the fish seemed to have deserted me completely. I was the fool sitting at one end, with a piece of mackerel dangling from the other. Michael Sugrue's customers were also slow to buy his line, and he was getting worried because there were no red sea bream to be had. He suggested we move to Ceann an Aonaigh, the Headland of the Fair, nearer to the rough ground, where we might find a school of sea bream. My father consented and proceeded to haul the anchor. We put out the oars once more, going farther to sea for about a half-mile, and cast anchor for the second time in much deeper water, my father remarking, 'If it's not for the better, let's hope it's not going to be for the worse.' Again we sent our lines to the bottom and to our delight, great red sea bream began to come in pairs over the side.

The fisherman must be careful to lift sea bream carefully out of the water and clear of the side of the boat. The lips of a sea bream are brittle and easily torn if the line is worked too vigorously as the fish pulls in the opposite direction. We were kept busy with the many bream and a mixed bag of other species. The unwelcome spiked dogfish would be dealt with in a brutal manner because of his dangerous fighting attitude, and kept within the boat while fishing was in progress. Another unwelcome guest was the speckled dogfish, infamous for its snake-like wriggling and its attempts to sandpaper the skin off your wrists when being taken from the hook. A small baton of hardwood was kept to render dogfish or small sharks unconscious: a few well-aimed blows of this baton across the navel of the fish was all that was needed. The baton was called the 'priest', and salmon fishermen also kept it to hand to administer the last rites, as salmon were known to leap into the sea after being brought on board. Some fishermen called it the 'clergyman' or the 'reverend parson'.

Michael Sugrue took the prize fish of the day, a small turbot of about eleven pounds. Using a small hook and light gear, Michael played the fish with unusual dexterity, while my father watched, gaff in hand, ready to bring it on board. My father would murmur, 'Easy, easy, Michael! Give him a bit of his own way; don't let him break you.' I enjoyed myself thoroughly and did not feel the time slipping by.

The last fish I brought on board was the middle species of red gurnard called the 'tub', whose flesh is not as tasty as that of the grey or red piper. I noticed my father furtively glancing towards the far horizon. Michael Sugrue exclaimed, 'What's troubling you, John?'

'Do you see that black wall appearing on the skyline? It seems to be approaching rapidly; maybe it is some kind of a sudden storm. However, we'll continue fishing while the going is good, and in the meantime we'll be ready in case we have to run for it,' my father answered.

He decided we would move closer to the land in case a sudden wind came up. We hove anchor once more and moved to within a quarter-mile of the shore. Three moves, they say, are as bad as a fire. This time my father got a huge conger eel on his line. He succeeded in bringing it up, but it was pull devil, pull baker, all the way from the bottom, until the fish finally broke the weaker snood on arriving at the surface. Watching the fish disappear, my father exclaimed, 'I hope you never come back – you are not a great loss to us.' The day was changing and the weather deteriorating rapidly. Large droplets fell plop into the sea once in a while. Small white clouds like balls of cotton wool came scurrying low from the direction of the Bull Rock, and we heard a rumble on the horizon ending in an ominous growl. It was the first bark of the coming storm.

We hauled anchor immediately, and put all our fish into a rod basket near the bow sheeting. The basket was overflowing with bream, whiting and codling. I bailed the boat free of surplus water and we clewed up our lines on their frames and made everything shipshape before pulling on our yellow home-made oilskin trousers. We put our cloth jackets into a sack in a dry place under the bow breast-hook, laid our oilskin jackets near at hand in case we might need them, got the oars into the water and

21

swung the boat before the south-west breeze, into a running position.

The storm was fascinating to watch, with the cloud layer becoming lower and more disturbed by the minute. I heard my father mutter, 'The wind will increase – we must hurry.' Shafts of lightning, like rivers of red liquid, stabbed the sea in front of the nearing storm. We kept up a steady long light stroke – easy work so far, running before the weather, but we had yet two miles and a half to cover, with the explosion of thunder and continuous rumbling as if from some fiery volcano in Hades. We were now approaching the Scéalaí Rock. The sky suddenly took fire above our heads, as a great bolt of light grounded on the hillside only yards above the cliff face, setting fire to the heather; the gulls screamed and scattered, while cormorants standing on the ledges disappeared beneath the water. Bolt after bolt entered the bay about a mile to our right. One blue streak of flame danced temporarily in front of our eyes, leaving us stupefied. My father stopped rowing, rubbed his eyes with the back of his knuckles and said, 'Oh Virgin! That was a near one!', though his face kept its usual placid expression. 'We'll make the Sign of the Cross,' he added, and reaching into the bows he produced a little bottle of Holy Water which he sprinkled on us in the name of the Holy Spirit. We continued to row eastward.

The force of the wind now made a worsening short-breaking sea. I saw a large plank of wood some distance off our beam, which I prayed God my father would not see, because he would risk life and limb to salvage it. But his gannet eye caught sight of it, and he ordered Michael Sugrue to swing the boat in its direction. We were now running in a following sea and brought the boat head to wind. My father lifted a fifteen-foot beam of pine from the water, pushed it gently under the thwarts, leaving some four feet protruding over the stern transom, remarking, 'Some more of those planks are in the currents, if only the weather was suitable to search for them.'

The white-caps were now like 'charging steeds' racing free and high; the lip of one caught us on the stern quarter and splashed harmlessly aboard. Soon my father made another change. He ordered me to stow my oar and Michael Sugrue rowed in the bow position with my father in the second berth. I was told to sit in the middle of the fourth seat with the bailing bucket on my lap, to keep the boat clear of any heavy water. The old master knew how to handle his small craft in a tormented sea. 'Row her long, light and steady! Let her rise, and only one way to run, run like the devil, from the break of a following sea, keep her perfectly straight on course, and above all don't let her fall across when she is planing on the crest of a wave.'

We were now running by the little headland of Cráiteach, which the seine fishermen nicknamed 'Greenland', because of its acre of tossed water. We avoided the worst by staying close to the cliff face where there is a deep channel. One heavy white-cap came half smashing over the side, spilling in about fifty gallons of water. I plied the bailing bucket furiously, in a continuous looping movement, so busy I didn't have time for butterflies in the gut. At last we ran through Horse Island Sound and into the shelter of the harbour, continued by the Rinn Dubh or Black Reef round by the head of Carraig, beaching the boat where we had started that morning. We sheltered under the ruined castle wall, for the storm had not yet lost its intensity and was spreading inland. My father forbade me to enter the castle, saying it was less dangerous standing in the shelter of the great outside wall, as lightning was known to follow air currents.

Some forked lightning streaked dangerously near into the waters of the beach, one flash in particular leaving a sulphurous stench like burning rubber. The wind continued to pull landwards, now blowing a full gale. Michael said, 'John! If we were out there now, we would surely be lost!'

My father replied, nonchalantly, 'Well, maybe! But Michael, you must always keep that "weather eye" open, and that is exactly what we did today: we were running away before the storm really got to us.'

Heavy squalls hit the length of the harbour, spiralling spray high into the air. We made the boat and gear secure, waiting for the weather to improve before hauling our nets, and my father and Michael divided a fine catch of fish between them. We were

welcomed home by my mother, who was getting anxious about
our safety. Our intention of making several trammel hauls in the
course of the day had been thwarted by the spectacular thunderstorm. Mike promised he would come at dawn to haul the nets.

Next morning dawned bright and fair. The bay looked like a
sheet of opal, streaked with azure. Hog's Head and Scariff Island
still wore collars of frilly surf, the residue of yesterday's angry
tempest. My mother was first out of bed and had the turf fire
blazing on the hearth. The old iron kettle gave occasional coughs
of steam, assuring us that it was about to boil over. She had
cooked half a dozen fresh hen eggs, the produce of her prized
Rhode Island Reds, the shells of which were a rich pink-brown.
My father had prepared thick cutlets of sea bream, which tasted
delicious with a sprinkle of salt and pepper and a knob of butter.
Mike Sugrue arrived and again we made our way to the beach,
eager to salvage our nets. We lost no time in getting the boat
afloat, taking a direct course to the Bay Rock. The marking buoys
were in the same position as we had set them the morning before.
I took small paddles to keep the boat clear of the nets while they
began hauling. The nets were, as old fishermen would say in
Irish, 'dirty' with fish, meaning that more fish than net were
visible. Michael and my father decided that the nets must be
stored carefully on the boat floor, to distribute the weight more
evenly. The catch included white and black pollack, many species
of crab from the great edible red crab to the velvet-back wader,
who is very handy at snipping meshes, and of course the notorious
spiked dogfish.

The last fish to be taken on board was a large conger eel, who
reacted violently to captivity and succeeded in tearing several
meshes and escaping on to the stern sheeting. My father had to
resort to the baton, administering the last rites and dropping the
eel into the sea. The hauling of the nets being finished with, we
headed back for the old castle beach.

It was good to watch my father and Michael produce their
tobacco pipes and light up, looking so happy after a job well
done. My father had a brown beard with whorls like Moses, now
streaked with grey. He was a tall man, a little over six feet, with

long Roman features. Michael Sugrue was tall, dark and good-looking, with a moustache. They both spoke soft musical Irish, in which they had a large vocabulary – many thousands of words each with its own distinct meaning. No word of English passed between those grand men of the past, who were proud of their Gaelic culture.

I was detailed to fetch the ass and cart with several home-made osier baskets while they stayed to clean the nets of fish. Our task done, we went homeward once more, and the fish were again divided.

Episodes such as this were part of my everyday life, and it was only much later that I became conscious of the debt I owed to these men who shared with me their knowledge and love of the sea, especially 'To My Father':

Only us both,
You and I,
With God
Up on high,
The wing
Of the gull,
The cloud,
The star
In the sky.
The soft surging
Seas,
The night
And a new dawn
In store.
The beacons
Are lighting us home
To Heaven's bright shore.

THE SKELLIGS

The Great Skellig, Sceilg Mhichíl, is situated nine miles west of Bolus Head. The rock is a mile in circumference, and more than seven hundred feet high. It consists mostly of grey-black slate, with mixtures of other rock; traces of white and red marble, brownstone, rock crystals, quartz and copper. Beautiful spires and turrets of rock, made by Nature's hand across aeons of time, give Skellig Michael an outline as majestic as a great cathedral. Sea pinks grow thick and heavy on the south-western side of the rock and offer shelter for nesting to the different species of sea-birds. Petrels, shearwaters and puffins burrow beneath the deep accumulation of turf-like soil, created by the centuries-long growth and decay of sea pinks and campion. These birds must go underground to avoid that most murderous predator, the great black-headed gull, whose own nest hangs precariously on a few inches of space, wedged in between hundreds of other nests. Arctic terns and kittiwakes scream plaintively, crying 'kittiwake, kittiwake', while the little auks stand like statues of graven stone, forever staring out to sea, seemingly oblivious to human presence.

A partly submerged reef runs south-westward from the Great Skellig, and shows in two jagged sections above the high-water line. The rocks are called The Women or Na Mná in Irish. This was a rich crayfish ground until teams of divers began to come with sophisticated equipment and put an end to shellfishing. The sea around the Skelligs was alive with different species of fish in my young days. May God be good to Paud Jack O'Sullivan, that king of fishermen: I wish him a little boat in some lovely harbour among the Isles of Heaven. I still seem to hear him say to me, 'A great place to wake in the morning, Michael, west of the Great Skellig.' Many a moonlit night we spent at anchor with our captain, Jim Fitzgerald, sleeping peacefully, our lobster traps ready for hauling at the dawning of a new day.

It was there, in the bosom of the ocean, that a community of Anchorite monks settled some time before the sixth century.

They raised stout, strong, sheltering walls of grey slatestone. Within those thick walls, seven hundred feet above sea level, they built a monastery of beehive stone cells culminating in a capstone with an aperture for smoke. The entire fabric was of dry stone without bonding mortar, yet the squared interiors were dry, airy and comfortable. The monastery today is as sound as when it was first built. Every priest or monk must have been an expert in building with stone: the labour and effort that went into the construction of the settlement can only be imagined. Within the enclosure are two springs of clear fresh water. Engineers say it is the pressure of the ocean that forces sea water upwards through porous rock, which filters out the salt. The monks are buried within a small mound. Over the grave of the abbot stands a great stone hewn to represent a cowled monk in his Mass vesture. Seven hundred steps of heavy footworn slabs lead up to the entrance in the monastery wall. Near the top, suspended between the northern and southern spires, is a bare valley-like gap called Christ's Saddle. According to local tradition, the hermits named it thus. The Blind Man's Cove is on the south side. Legend has it that a blind man from Ballinskelligs asked to be landed there, then crawled on his knees up the entire pathway until he reached the monastery, where the light was miraculously restored to his eyes.

The great spire of Skellig is on the western shoulder of the rock. The monks chiselled crude footholds into the cliff which leans out over the sea. Dangerous steps and rock barriers lead up to an opening in the cliff face called the Needle's Eye. After you pass through the Eye, you go to the highest point, called the Stone of Penance, which leans out 718 feet over the depths below. The stone itself is shaped like a horse's back, and ten feet out a cross is carved at the end. Fearless pilgrims scramble out and kiss the cross, with nothing below them but the blue ocean. This is not for the squeamish. Yet it is said only one person ever fell to his death – one who had mocked at the idea of a spiritual pilgrimage.

Tradition locates the grave of Irr, son of Milesius, on the Great Skellig, where he received Christian baptism when his ship was wrecked on the rock. Skellig Michael was dedicated to the Arch-angel Michael. St Finan is said to have established canons of St

Augustine on the rock. The *Annals of Loch Léin* record the 'repose' of Flann Macallach, Abbot of Great Skellig, in the year 885, and of Blathmac Sgellice in 950. A third abbot, Aed, 'chief of the Gael in piety', died in 1044.

The monks used boats of frame and leather. Great oxskins were tanned with the juice of the oak bark, then sewn on to the light frames of oak and ash. When the boat was finished, the leather was smeared with mutton fat.

A treacherous reef called the Monks' Rock lies under water on the south side of Skellig Michael. It is said that the monks' *naomhóg* was wrecked there one day with the loss of some lives, and the monks carved a Christian cross on the reef. A strange formation of rock stands overlooking the reef. This is called Bean an Uaill or The Wailing Woman. On the western side the monks carved two heads, one male, one female, representing Adam and Eve, gazing forward towards the far horizon.

Tourists come from many parts of the world to visit Skellig Michael. Some have a special interest in Celtic culture, and in the archaeology of the period of early monasticism. It is also a delightful place for the student of bird life.

One day during the 1930s Jim Fitzgerald and I took two ladies to the Skellig. They had hired the boat for an agreed sum. Mother and daughter of a distinguished family, they were intensely interested in archaeology, and had done a world tour to look at antiquities. They had come from Istanbul to Ireland to see the Great Skellig, on their way back to America. The mother told me how she had listened to the late Professor James Delargy deliver a lecture in Chicago about ancient Irish culture. In his lecture he spoke of the Great Skellig – its monastic life, its beehive colony of stone cells, its beauty and its bird life. On hearing the lecture she decided she must see it at some future date.

On arriving at the rock, Jim Fitzgerald stayed with the boat while I accompanied the women as their guide. It was a warm summer evening – a perfect setting to reward the tourists for their long journey. The sky was a hazy blue and the ocean beneath a mirror of tinted blue glass with the various sea-birds floating in space. We had arrived near Christ's Saddle, not far from the entrance to the monastery, when the mother stopped suddenly, telling me that she could not go on. I saw that she was frightened, though I assured her there was no danger. She told her daughter to go on alone and see the monastery. I got her seated on a great smooth slab of slate, and stayed with her. I talked to her about the folklore of the Skelligs and I noticed she became more comfortable and relaxed. She then told me the cause of her anxiety. Some years previously she and her husband had been in Mexico climbing up the steps of an Aztec sun temple, when her husband suddenly collapsed and died of a heart attack. Both places seemed so strikingly similar in structure that she imagined she saw for a fleeting moment the entire sad scene of her husband's death. Mother and daughter assured us they enjoyed the trip, despite the emotional setback.

Another lady visited Ballinskelligs in the year 1938. She had a doctorate from a university in Germany and had permission to travel among the Irish people collecting folklore and taking photographs. She wanted to visit the Great Skellig and include it in her writings, although she made no secret of her revulsion for Christianity and constantly mocked the idea of a Supreme Being. Her argument was that all was chance, but she took umbrage when I remarked that if this were so we were all included in the word chance, which reduced us to being born chancers. The astonishing thing was that she always kept in her pocket a brass talisman like a little monkey, and although she dismissed the idea of God, she believed her talisman had mysterious powers. She kept repeating, 'My talisman will keep me from harm.'

The weather was broken and unsettled. A great heavy sea and severe surf prevented us from making the trip for two weeks, and in the meantime she took photographs of pilgrims at St Michael's Shrine on Pattern day saying the Rosary around the well. She thought these people were deranged. In the end the weather cleared and we made the trip to the Great Skellig the next Sunday. She was anxious to see the monastic settlement and to write about it.

We had several tourists with us on the same trip. Jack Fitzgerald was our skipper and Miss Fenton, the Ballinskelligs national school teacher, and myself were with the German lady. We started to climb the flagged pathway up to the monastery, and it wasn't long before we noticed our German doctor sinking slowly to the ground, complaining of feeling faint. Jack Fitzgerald and myself seated her at the point we had started out from, and gave her some refreshments. She quickly recovered and expressed her desire to attempt the journey upwards once again. After a short rest to restore her energy – in Irish, 'the rest of the blacksmith's boy: from the anvil to the bellows' – we continued once more, and everything went fine until we reached the place where she had fallen before. It was fortunate that we were walking by her side, for this time she asked to be taken down again, saying that both her legs were paralysed. It was true for her – they seemed to have no feeling or movement. With the assistance of the other boatmen we took her bodily to the roadway where she immediately walked. That ended her chance of ever seeing the monastery. She told us that her experience was most strange, in so far as she was not afraid of heights. One old fisherman's verdict on what had happened made us all laugh: 'Don't you know the holy monks in heaven wouldn't let that bitch into the monastery!'

We came home that evening. The learned doctor had nothing to relate about her trip to the Great Skellig: no photographs, no notes – perhaps the little brass monkey had taken the day off. She told me she was not going back to Germany because she said a world war was imminent. She left Ballinskelligs the next day.

Some months afterwards Miss Fenton got a letter from a friend living in Toronto, enclosing a copy of a supplement from a Canadian newspaper. Under the name of the learned German doctor the newspaper carried a headline in large print: 'The land of St Patrick as it is today, a land of devilry and laughter.' A photograph of the schoolteacher's aged mother, Nora Roche, saying her Rosary in the garden, was accompanied by the words: 'This old woman carries a Rosary beads but utters the words of a spell.' Another picture of praying at St Michael's Shrine carried the caption: 'They still worship water in a so-called Christian land.' Under a picture of children was written: 'Barefoot Irish maidens laugh easily.' I don't want to splash more water on drowned mice.

I'll reveal nothing more about the learned doctor who was granted licence by the authorities to walk among my people and who wrote scurrilously about them. May her spirit climb the stairway to Paradise without fear or emotion, and the Holy Anchorites welcome her to the eternal city. And on her way up may she cast from her that little idol of a brass monkey!

*   *   *

Little Skellig, situated half-way between the Great Skellig and Lomán Rock, is a wild, spiky, splintered rock formation, hard to climb because of the huge slabs of rotting slate that slip down on the sloping cliff face. Many days and nights I spent fishing the reefs and caves for great blue lobster and crayfish with the Fitzgeralds, Jack and Jim. You need a fine day for lobster fishing around this rock. To the north-west the ground is rough and uneven, with several sunken reefs which are dangerous in rough weather. Strong ocean currents run on high tides, making it difficult to haul lobster gear. Herds of grey Atlantic seals can be seen on the rocks as the tide goes out, including great bulls whose weight must be close to half a ton. They especially like the heat of a midsummer's day.

But it was not fishing I intend to write about now, but how I became interested in sea-birds. It happened that a woman ornithologist was commissioned by the British government to carry out a count of the sea-birds around the coast of the British Isles. She was equipped with all kinds of cameras for both prints and slides. After completing a survey of the Faroe Islands she was now to survey the Little Skellig and had asked to be put ashore on the rock when the weather was suitable. The rock itself is not easy to step ashore on, with no steps or jetty but the slippery deceiving cliff face. On that particular day, Jim Fitzgerald, John Peter O'Shea, myself and the bird woman set out, towing astern a twenty-foot rowing boat attached to a stout cable. By the time we reached the rock the weather was rapidly deteriorating: sheep's fleece in the sky, the breeze quickening from the south-west, and a look of rain in the eye of the morning sun. The captain told me I was to accompany the lady up among the birds. I can truthfully say that I was not eager to face up that frowning cliff. I was burdened with a haversack sixty pounds in weight, and got strict orders not to fall, because the gear was worth a small fortune. The lady then instructed me how I should conduct myself among the birds, and she herself put on a pair of special climbing shoes. We boarded our craft to approach the surf-bound cliff and chose a suitable landing place after anchoring the big boat in deep water away from the rock. Then Jim Fitzgerald and John O'Shea rowed us towards the landing point. An old Irish saying could well be applied here. 'Study the river, lest you enter the whirlpool.'

After searching for some time we found a place with deep water and a broad sloping slab of flat rock. The bird woman was six foot three inches tall and broad in the beam as well, God bless her – a miniature Amazon. She had boasted to me that if she were young again she could run up the face of that rock. We were both standing on the stern sheeting, waiting for Jim Fitzgerald's order: he had told us that when he said the word 'Go!' we were to obey his command at once because of the great rise and fall of the breaking surf. He held the boat steady for seconds with the oar blades thrust deep in the churning sea. After hearing the signal we found ourselves standing safely on the rock.

Losing no time, we climbed outward to the level of the bird colony, but the terrain became more difficult, until at last it was clear that we were already trapped. I took off the cumbersome haversack and wellingtons and searched for a way forward, in my stockinged feet. The slippery rock where we stood did not afford very safe ground, for it slanted abruptly at about fifty degrees towards the sea. The only escape route which presented itself was a narrow fissure, not much wider than a toe-hold, which led to a larger platform of rock above our heads. To reach the gap in the cliff face we would have to crawl across a narrow ledge of rock, there to stand upright to pull and squeeze through the gap. I went first, pushing the haversack ahead, and succeeded in getting through safely. She came next, not running but crawling carefully, and when she stood upright I grasped her right hand and hauled her up into the narrow gap to safety. One time when I had exerted more pressure than she could bear, she entreated me not to break her arm. She was getting on in years, and not so nimble any more.

The climb became less difficult from then on, and in a short while we were surrounded by birds, thousands of great gannets on their nests all around us. We sat on a rock without stirring or speaking. It was wonderful to watch these ferocious creatures only inches away, showing no fear, no interest in our presence. Her instructions were to ignore the birds and move very slowly. We chose a vantage point for the camera and during the next hour she took photographs of the different areas. She also had a map of the rock. For me, that day among the birds was an education in Nature's own university.

She spoke about the habits of the different species of sea-birds on the coast of Ireland, explaining and teaching as she continued to work. She was a fluent talker, and easily understood. She spoke about gulls, large, medium and small, the great diving birds, the gannets or Solan geese, crossbills, razorbills, guillemots, auks, terns, Arctic terns, puffins, petrels, black sea witch and fulmar petrels, Manx shearwater petrels, the great Northern diver which in Irish is called the *lóma*, rock pipits, blue rock pigeons, choughs, cormorants, and the green shag. She awakened in me such a great interest in bird life that later I bought some books on the subject and studied them. There was a rich smell of guano: every nook and cranny was overflowing with rank manure, dead remains of fish, chicks and eggshells. Neighbouring mothers could be seen stealing pieces of precious nesting material from one another. The clamour of the different tones blending with the raucous 'craak, craak' of thousands of gannets, together with the booming of surf in the caves and the rising wind, gave us the signal that it was time to depart. We packed all the gear into the haversack, which was once more strapped on my back. We proceeded downwards until we came to the difficult part we had met on our way up. I eased myself down carefully until I found with my feet the narrow ledge beneath, where I stood upright and told her to face in and lower her body very carefully down.

I stretched my arms above me until I got both my palms under the cheeks of her buttocks, just as she would sit on a chair. I helped her slowly downwards. Once I glanced fearfully upwards, to see for a fleeting moment the whole weight of the ornithological department (in the broadest posterior sense), appearing to descend upon me like a great parachutist clad in black knickers. It was a miracle that the weighty Saxon female and myself came safely off the dangerous cliff face. At one point one of her shoes became wedged in the rock: I might not have lived to tell the tale had she not torn her foot from it. The shoe detached itself and sailed over our heads down into the sea below. I pulled on my wellingtons and we both made for the boat. The men guided it gently into a perfect position, and on Jim's order, we were aboard in a flash. Experience is the best teacher. If you ever go climbing, take a rope along.

The bird woman estimated that more than twenty thousand gannets were on the Skellig that year, among several other species. We were happy that the trip was over as the weather got steadily worse, with white surf like a collar of lace around the Little Skellig. I got two pounds extra for being her guide. Two pounds was hard to come by in those days.

The following is a translation of my Irish poem describing a fisherman's first visit to Skellig Michael.

I visited Skellig Michael
Today,
A fisherman
Without homespun
Cowl or tonsure,
Book or beads
Between fingers,
Listening dumbfounded
To flagstones
Telling
Of a Nazarene,
The Carpenter's Son,
Who from death
Had risen.
The kittiwakes
In the cave
Saying

'We were here then!
We are here still!
Do you remember
The dark night
Of plunder,
The clamour
And the boom
Of the Northmen's
Great oars
Coming on the wind?
And the Danes
Without mercy
Raving for loot?
Over the wave
From the East
Came sea robbers,
Their bald prows
And shielded gunwales
Concealing
Battle-axe and spear.'

Humble Anchorites,
Your ravaged cells
Are prayerless tonight,
But flagstones
Whisper yet,
And kittiwakes
In the cave.

My native village is forever linked with Skellig of the Shadows: it is called Ballinskelligs and our parish of Prior derives its name from the priory of St Michael's Abbey, once renowned as a seat of learning. A saying is still heard which is as old as the abbey itself: 'Better a week in the priory than a year at school.' Canons Regular of St Augustine were the last to occupy the abbey. The last abbot was called Blowick, a name not common in the locality.

The late Professor Delargy searched universities on the Continent for information about the abbey and the castle by the sea. He discovered very little, so we have to fall back on local lore handed down for generations. All we have otherwise are the broken walls, and a silent chasm in so far as written history is concerned. There is not a whisper of information about when the monks were forced from Skellig Michael – it is thought that the Church reformer St Malachy of Bangor visited during his exile in 'Ibraceuse' in the 1120s and that the Augustinians took over from the Anchorites – or how many years it took to build the once great monastery at Ballinskelligs. The priory had many rooms and chapels, even streets and houses whose foundations can still be seen. As many buildings again vanished through sea erosion. Many questions can't be answered. Why were there no monks' graves in the monastery garden here, but only on Skellig itself? Where did the monks go? What happened to the books they wrote? What became of their sacred vessels that not a single artefact from that time was ever found? Some say that the religious community survived into the 1630s, but I fear this breach in our history will stay forever covered by the cold grave-slab.

At a point between the castle and the monastery, which was once a green field near the shore, there showed a long narrow hollow. One morning after a great storm the sea exposed the front of the field, and it was full of skeletons and skulls, each cut in front as if by axe or sword. I heard my father say there were scores of skulls in a common grave. Were those the remains of the monks who once occupied the Priory of Ballinskelligs?

II

Seed-Time and Harvest

KELP AND POTATOES

My brother Paddy awakened me at daybreak. Giving me a gentle shake, he said, 'Get up! Patas Curran and I are going west to the island sound for a boatload of stripe to manure the potatoes. We will need you to keep the boat free from water.'

On hearing this, I jumped out of my warm bed, knowing I would not have to attend school. I hated school, anyway. I was now eleven years old, tall, with spindly legs, barefooted and bare-headed. My mother objected, but Paddy impressed on her the importance of my job, which was to bail out water which would be taken on board with the kelp. My mother advised Paddy not to overload the boat, and to distribute the seaweed evenly. Before we departed she gave us her blessing, and sprinkled us with Holy Water. I carried a gallon canister and a tin bucket for bailing the boat.

Patas Curran was waiting for us on the beach, the great crooked sickle with its long handle on his shoulder. The kelp-cutting sickle is a blunt instrument. Were it too sharp it would not bring the kelp to the surface in the loop of its mouth. The boat was near the pier, a four-oar craft, twenty-five feet long. It was built by 'Pardner' Galvin, who was expert at building a seaworthy and shapely boat. An old fisherman christened her the *Glassy Gander* and the name stuck. When we went on board Paddy took up the stern sheeting to inspect the water plug in the bilge. The tide was still ebbing, and the sea was like a sheet of opaque glass. This was the great spring tide: it would not reach out so far again until autumn. Patas pulled on the bow oar, while my brother rowed in the second berth. Under both oars, the *Glassy Gander* moved easily westward, like a phantom floating on air.

This was the life I loved, the freedom of the sea and the smell of salt, phosphorous and iodine. The morning sun shone into the Cave of the Rock Doves on our right, producing a roseate enamel blending with tints of pink and light purple. It was as if I were looking through a giant kaleidoscope. Who would be imprisoned in a musty schoolroom on a morning such as this?

The oarsmen changed course, to avoid the light ground or shallow on the shoulder of Mike Shea's reef. A large area of drowning man's laces covered the shallow part of the Sound. It was impossible to row between the long matted sea strings which grew long and dense. A swimmer in this area would have no chance of survival. Still, it was a good position for mooring a trammel net, for the mullet and sea bass were often found in abundance among the sea strings. Sea trout also like to swim among the cords. Of course it was unlawful for us to catch a young salmon or sea trout when fishing for mullet. Even though we didn't invite the fish to get caught in mullet meshes, it was a crime to keep or eat illegally caught fish of this description, and perhaps we were also in danger of hell-fire, so like good Christians we always put them back where they came from.

We slipped silently to the left of Carraig an Phollóig, the Pollack Rock. The water was receding quickly, so the jagged sunken reef of the Sound was showing. The double-headed kelp and the great black sea rods, some broken and naked after the winter storms, pushed their heads above the water. We were now floating on top of a vast submarine forest. The water rose and fell as the round heads of the sea rods appeared momentarily above the surface. We could have filled several boats with them, but were only interested in the long yellow ribbon kelp and in the heavy belted dark brown stripe, which grew long and slender. We also cut the short-stemmed whip kelp and the serrated kelp. My brother and Patas brought the boat into a fixed position near the reef where the side was fair and deep. They divested themselves of their woollen *geansaí* and of their inside shirts and put on sleeveless jackets and old trousers.

Each took turns at the cutting sickle, one bringing great armfuls of brown kelp to the surface while the other took the long streamers from the mouth of the crooked sickle. Much water was taken on board with the dripping weed. I managed to keep the main floor of the boat bailed. Paddy was the architect responsible for distributing the kelp evenly. Each armful he laid carefully in its place, making it flat and laying it clockwise, just as in making a rick of hay. The *Gander* settled lower into the water under the weight of the cargo of black-brown velvet streamers which we had won from the unpolluted waters. We now had little more than six inches of freeboard to spare, but the sea was calm as glass.

My brother Paddy said we had taken enough on board. Patas jumped onto a flat rock by our side, taking the tin bucket with him, and choosing a suitable piece of stone, he began to chip loose the great flat *bairneachs* or limpets which are seldom exposed to the sunlight. This limpet is related to the 'Chinese hat', and is not tidal. It has a pale buttery colour, is fat and makes an excellent soup. In no time he had collected nearly a pailful of them, which he gave to me as a gift. Paddy kept the boat steady until Patas came on board. The tide had now turned to flow while they rowed the *Gander* gently by Cloigeann an Chrainn. With the kelp stowed high and square over her gunwale, she resembled a Venetian gondola as we berthed safely at the pier. The harvest provided enough fertilizer to nourish the potato crop for that year, and the memory of that happy morning remains with me still, even though more than seventy years have flown. My brother and Patas have now passed over the divide. May they rest in peace, Patas in the Old Priory burial-ground, which was once St Michael's Abbey, and my brother Paddy in a cemetery beneath the lovely hills of Connecticut, U. S. A.

The potato plot was treated with a liberal coating of sea kelp, which was in plentiful supply along the south-western coast where it was cast ashore by the winter storms. When mixed with farm-yard manure, the decayed residue of winter bedding of cattle housed in the byre, this fertilizer was rich in mineral elements, making it an excellent dressing for potatoes. Most of the work on the smallholdings was done with a special iron spade which could be bought in any ironmonger's store. It was sold in separate parts: the iron spade, the treadle, and the ash handle. The parts would be taken to an experienced joiner, who carefully assembled the parts to suit the workman, right or left-handed as the case might be. A good spade worker would plant a bed of potatoes one hundred yards long by three feet wide each day. It was slow, laborious work, but by this method more potatoes were produced on the smallholdings than on some of the larger estates. The small cottiers did not keep horses and therefore did not have ploughs.

Many varieties of potato were grown. An early variety which survived the blight of the Great Famine was a round dark purple-skinned potato called the 'stouter'. This would be ready for the table in mid-May. In my youth anybody worth his salt would have cultivated a bed of early 'stouters'. The main crop was a yellow-fleshed tuber called 'champion'; this was a dry floury potato with a very sweet taste. Housewives described them when boiled as bursting their jackets with goodness. Another long tuber was called the 'peeler'. This was a soft and soapy white potato, easily cultivated and used mostly for animal feeding.

The potato fields were a pretty sight when seen in full blossom, after being earthed and manured with guano, a powerful fertilizer imported from the Pacific and South Atlantic. A strong solution of sulphate of copper mixed with soda crystals made a forty-gallon barrel of wash. The knapsack sprayer was not yet on the market, so in those early years we sprayed with little hand brooms, taking the wash in an open bucket and walking through the furrows. This was a crude method, but it kept at bay the dreaded fungus spores which attacked the potato holms.

GROWING FLAX

About the year 1875 my mother was sixteen years old. She told me that flax was sown and grown in the locality in plentiful supply, and that there was no lovelier sight than the small fields of blue blossom in full bloom. From her I heard the story of its growing and processing. Some of the information, alas, is gone, because it never occurred to me that the wasp should ever goad me so deeply in later life that I would plough a blank field of parchment and seed it with my thought.

Flax was easily grown. It required little fertilizer, or else the crop would grow too rank and produce too much soft bark on the stem. A flax which had no commercial value was called 'the flax of the fairy women'. People would have nothing to do with this, and it was considered a bad omen to have it growing among the good crop.

When the blossom faded the flax ripened into seed and became fit for reaping. The seed was taken out with little flails made for the purpose. Linseed oil was used for the relief of constipation in farm animals. Meal was also made from the seed and fed to young calves.

Each farmer had his own special pond of fresh water in which the sheaves were soaked, until the outer hard skin became soft and brittle. The flax was then taken from the pond to be placed on a wooden bench, where the sheaves drip-dried. The stems were beaten gently with a wooden mallet to crack the bark, and the sheaves once more opened and spread under the sun to dry. At this stage the *sistealóir* or flax dresser took over. He had special instruments, such as the flax comb, the hackle and the tongs, and removed the now-brittle bark, the cockle, and any other rough growth, without damaging the core of silvery threads. He prepared the flax for spinning, and there was plenty of demand for his skills as he travelled from village to village.

Because flax looked so much like the silken tresses of women, a traditional system of measuring was devised. One handful of unspun flax was a *scoithín*, or lock of hair, twelve handfuls or locks equalled one tress, or *treisleán*, and twelve tresses made one ball of twine weighing one pound and some ounces. This was a crude yet effective measurement. A special spinning wheel used for flax was called the fast wheel, or *luaidhaire*. Many Irish poems referred to flax. The speaker in this poem is a woman whose lover is going to the wars:

> *I'll sell my rock and I'll sell my reel*
> *And sell my only spinning-wheel.*
> *I spun the flax and I sold it well*
> *I bought for my love a sword of steel.*

Hempen twine was homespun. The women knitted fishing nets for coarse bottom fishing of hake and various other fish. The thread was coarse but hard-wearing. Weavers made clothing from it but it was cold to the touch and it never ousted woollen fabric from the market.

CUTTING THE TURF

Today very few people in Ballinskelligs use the traditional turf spade called a *sleán*. The machine is now doing the work of the *meitheal*, a working party of neighbours who helped each other to harvest a winter's fuel. Now you must buy turf from the person who owns the bogland – if you have the two or three hundred pounds you need in your fist. As the Gaelic poet said about money:

> *A fool can keep me,*
> *A wise man may spend me,*
> *Gather some of me,*
> *And you will have a lot of me.*

Money did not count during the turf harvest when I was young. Neighbours always helped each other. There were acres of bogland in every locality along South Iveragh. Each family from Cahersiveen to Bolus had its own turfbank. The fuel was of very good quality, dense, dark and brown. For an annual rent of between ten shillings and two pounds, you could cut enough turf for a year. Woe to him who could not provide enough turf for the winter's fire, for that individual was either bone lazy or not worth his salt. In Gaelic tradition a fire was as important as food, and saving the winter's turf was a very important job. In the poem 'Raca Breá Mo Chinn', or 'My Beautiful Head Comb' the maiden entreats a young man to marry her in the following words:

> *'It is a good time to marry,*
> *My young boy,' said she,*
> *'Ere the rest of the harvest comes,*
> *And we will have stored the turf.'*

Uneasy would be the man of the house until the turf was cut. Each man in the community gave a day's work for a day in return. People were friendly, kindly neighbours, who liked to be in partnership not alone on the day of the turf-cutting but at any time of urgent necessity.

I remember how stirred with joy we were when turf-cutting day came around. We did not have to go to school that day. The lunch basket was all packed the night before. My mother would prepare large oven-baked loaves, plenty of hen eggs, fresh butter and sweet jam, a big can of spring water, a can of fresh milk, the big kettle, and two ounces of plug tobacco as a gift for the pipe-smokers. The turf pikes, the *sleán* and the ordinary garden spades and shovels were all ready long since, and the local men notified. There was no fear of any man ignoring his neighbour's *meitheal,* unless something urgent prevented his attendance.

Four men usually followed each *sleán*: the man who was cutting, the man who took the sods, called the brincher, the man on the brink of the trench, and a fourth who spread the sods to dry. It was good to watch them working in unison, with no fear of wasted, broken or trampled turf.

The first thing we did on reaching the turfbank was to choose a sheltered place where the lunch could be prepared for the workmen. A great glowing turf fire was lit, the kettle was brought to the boil, with several teapots brewing and a small pot with perhaps a score of eggs inside bubbling on the live coals. Brown and white loaves were cut into thick slices, which some men plastered with great blobs of home-churned butter. The men could eat as many eggs as they requested, and would wash down the meal with big mugs of sweetened tea. After feasting, the team would rest for some time on the gorse and heather sward, and as they resumed their work one could hear the rasping noise from emissions of superfluous gas:

> *It is a good horse that will fart at noon time*
> *But it is a better horse who will fart at eventide*
> *And better is the work which causes the horse to fart.*

As evening approached, the heath was covered with an array of turf sods neatly spread, each cube lying on the shoulder of its neighbour, waiting for wind and summer sun to make it ready for next winter's fuel.

When the last sod was cut and the task complete, the men looked with satisfaction at the work they had all taken part in. The man of the house would then address them, saying he wished them God's blessing and not as much as a germ of sickness in the years to come. The answer always came back 'that the wish may also be yours'. A man who has never heard that loving wish after a day's co-operation with his neighbour is the poorer for it.

The sound of the modern machine can now be heard on Réidh na gCúl, on Currach na nDamh and at Gob an Dá Chaol. The raw smell of diesel oil comes easy on the wind. There are only three men now where once there were twenty. The machine has no conscience, no faith, no soul – it is a cold, serious, business-like master, interested only in profit. A new Caesar with a heart as cold as iron has taken the turf-cutting away from the *meitheal.* Caesar must be paid, or it is with the 'fire of the fox' – '*tine an mhadra rua*' – that the old and feeble will have to face the winter.

An ancient Irish folk-tale tells how one frosty morning a vixen and her cubs were travelling across barren land. The cold and hungry cubs were bewailing the intense cold, until Mother Fox urinated on an icy flagstone. A white vapour rose into the morning air, whereupon the cubs stopped complaining and huddled together around the source of heat, and Mother Fox was heard to say, 'Hush! my beauties, we shall soon have a fire.' And so a green or slow fire is still referred to as the 'fire of the fox'.

OATS AND HAY

I remember seeing my father and our neighbour Pat O'Connell reap a three-quarter-acre field of oats with sickle hooks about seventy years ago. In the morning before they set out to reap, they tied makeshift pads to their knees. It was fascinating to watch how rapid was their progress, and how skilled they were in the use of the sickle. One reaper moved a few yards ahead of the other and they laid the oats in perfect rows, ready for binding. I tried my hand at using the reaping hook, only to inflict a nasty cut on my little finger, the mark of which is plainly visible to the present day. Later on the scythe came onto the market with its long crooked wooden handle, mounted and turned by the local blacksmith. The scythe blades were manufactured in Sheffield from steel of excellent quality, honed and ground. They were razor-sharp and would slice through the long grass, when used by an expert. Good mowers would cut an acre of hay per day for the princely sum of ten shillings. The scythe was sharpened with a flat piece of wood, eighteen inches long and three inches wide, whose sides were coated with emery grains cemented to the wood. These pieces were called scythe-boards and sold for sixpence. In later years the more expensive carborundum sharpening-stone was imported from England. The modern version of the scythe is sold in a ready-to-assemble pack, complete with iron tubular handle. It is a handy instrument for the lawn gardener, but not for mowing an acre of hay per day.

Making hay was laborious work in the old days, especially if there was broken showery weather which might delay the drying process. The first little heaps were called grasscocks. The young folk who were being trained in the art of making the perfect grasscock were exhorted to put only the minimum amount of grass into its construction. I heard of one old farmer who lost his patience with his pupils and said in desperation: 'I want you to make the grasscocks only just about the size of a hen's shit. Now can you understand?'

The next stage was a larger cock which would contain a couple of hundredweight of hay. Those cocks were allowed to age for several days before being spread out under wind and sun until the hay was perfectly dry, to be made into what were called 'wynds'.

A wynd or meadowcock had to be properly made. It would contain about a half-ton of hay. Then came the final day for the great haggard cocks. The haggard enclosure would be cleared of any nettles or other growth, and the stone foundation where the great conical ricks were to be built made exact in circumference, and raised above the ground level.

The great storecock would contain as many as twenty-five meadow wynds – eleven or twelve tons of hay. The cock would taper outwards and upwards, until it reached its greatest circum-- ference, which would be in the region of fifty feet. From this point it became slowly conical, culminating in a point like an inverted spinning-top. It was imperative that the hay be perfectly dry to prevent pressure heating or fermentation. To construct a storecock of these dimensions would need at least ten workmen. Three experienced men worked in the rick, and three more on the ground kept them supplied with great forkfuls of hay. The men in the rick laid and distributed the hay, layering it evenly in a clockwise direction, making sure that the great centre was kept very solid underfoot with no humps or hollows. Two neighbours with horse carts drew loads from the meadows to keep the haggard in good supply, and with them would be two others who filled the loads and helped tie the ropes. One man had the most onerous job of all: his task was to keep the outer wall in perfect geometric balance. This man was the architect whose experienced eye over-saw the whole operation.

A good dinner would be laid on and, as it was thirsty work, the men would be supplied at intervals with a drink of black por-ter. Those workers were usually in serious mood when construct-ing the big top of hay, for each wanted it to be the showpiece of the neighbourhood. The housewife would have prepared a cap of sackcloth with which to cover the point of the rick from rain. The last job was the raking down of all loose or surplus hay and the tying with red fibre ropes spaced at eighteen-inch intervals. When the hay forks and hay rakes were finished with for the season they were laid carefully away, perhaps on the cross-rafters of the cow byre, until next year.

The first horse-drawn mowing machines did not reach Ballin-skelligs until the early twenties. This machine was manufactured in Ireland, as was also the old hand-turned chopping and pulping machine. In the late nineteen-forties I saw a reaping and binding machine for the first time in the 'beautiful vale of Tralee' and some years later the first threshing machine began operating in South Iveragh.

White and black oats were grown successfully in Ballinskelligs. Great circular stacks with thatched tops were to be seen in every haggard. The great problem was to get at the grain, as it had to be threshed by hand. Our forefathers were trained in the use of the flail stick, but this was before my time.

On the smallholdings I have described, grain was fed to the cattle on the sheaf. Mixed with hay, it provided good winter fodder. Barley and rye were grown in smaller quantities, because certain soils contained too much lime to grow oats successfully. The average smallholding was less than twenty acres, and in most cases, half of this was not arable. The fields on each holding were reduced to small half-acre paddocks. They were usually surrounded by fences of clay, stone and grass about six feet high, with a hedge of French furze on top. In springtime the French furze was topped with yellow blossom which presented a pretty sight on the green landscape and also provided shelter for the little fields. The seed for this furze was imported from France where it was cultivated because of its high protein content, and was considered good animal feed. The Irish used it more for shelter hedges than for fodder, although I have seen it used in chopped form as feed for horses. In South Iveragh, French furze left unattended grew wild, but with the advent of modern farming it was uprooted and destroyed.

The following is a translation from my Irish poem called 'The Harvest Moon':

How beautiful
The harvest moon
Spinning silver silk
In every glen;
Moonbeams mingle
While rich swathes
Slumber within
Their stubbled beds.

Come! let us go,
To where great ricks

Are making,
Where golden sheaves
Are garnered
For the grain;
Tonight we feast
The festival
Of the reaping,
And dance
With elves
Beneath the harvest moon.

THE GENTLEMAN AT HOME

Taking the cow to the bull was a hush-hush exercise. I was twelve years old when my father asked me to help him with an unruly cow which happened to come to dairy. When my mother's reluctant approval was granted, I was allowed for the first time to witness one of nature's oldest rituals, that of fertility, in a practical form.

The cow was in a heated frenzy. An otherwise placid animal now refused to lead, walk, run, or be drawn. She swung round and round in circles, backed, sulked and bellowed. My father walked ahead with a lead rope while I took up the rear, striking the cow every now and again with a slender willow rod. After what seemed an eternity, we finally reached the farmyard of Tom 'the bull'. Tom greeted my father, and asked the necessary questions. When did the animal have its last calf? When did it show signs of heat? Tom went into a back yard where he opened a gate, calling out at the top of his voice, 'Jack! Jack! Jack! Wuarra! Wuarra! Wuarra!' To my amazement, Jack, a cross between shepherd and collie, appeared and came trotting after his master, who was armed with a stout pitchfork.

The bull was magnificent: black as coal, broad-backed with a gleaming coat. Unlike the square ferocious-looking cross-bred bulls, this beast had class, of the pure Kerry breed. It snorted and shook its majestic head violently, as if in scorn of us mere humans. The front shoulders were broad, muscular and deep, while the dewlap hung low from its throat like a black velvet drape. One half of the horns was cream-coloured and pointed, looping out and upwards. The animal seemed to exude a savage virility.

The cow turned around, sniffing at the handsome gentleman in his black glossy suit. I think she even approved of their meeting, as she gave him a few licks of her long curling tongue under the ear. With sudden and decisive intensity, and that inborn, primordial power whose object is the renewal of the species, the drama reached its climax. It all happened in such a short time: one wild leap and lunge, and in less than ten seconds, Nature had taken its course. Tom 'the bull' gave the signal to take the cow away. The bull would have followed us but Tom, complete with pitchfork and his faithful friend, had already herded the animal back into its own quarters. This was my first experience of procreation. Later on, when I grew older, I had the responsibility of taking matters in my own hands. There is an old saying in Irish: 'The man who owns a cow must be responsible for a cow.'

One day when I was taking my cow to be served, I approached the farm where the bull was kept. The animal must have anticipated our arrival. The huge Hereford monster broke loose from the paddock where it was kept, and galloped towards me, head lowered in menace, copper ring in its nose. I tried to put the cow between myself and the mountain of horned beef bearing down on us, but the cow panicked and with the excess pressure the leading rope parted. The cow turned tail and raced homewards. I also turned tail and fled towards the farmhouse. I succeeded in leaping over a low sod fence, and into the farmer's field. The bull leaped clumsily, sending green scraws of turf in all directions, as I scrambled over the fence once more and on to the roadway. I gained more ground towards the farmhouse which was about fifty yards distant and ran for my life towards a dry wall of rough fieldstone that surrounded the back yard, my heart pounding, my breath coming in short gasps. The rough stone wall was nearly six feet high and I could feel the brute breathing down my shirt collar. He stood on the outside glowering at me, pulling clods of earth with the pawing of his front hooves and deftly throwing them skyward. Thank God! the back door opened, the farmer's daughter saw what was happening and she alerted her mother. The good woman explained that her husband was at the fair and said I was to be sure and bring back the cow that evening. She told me that the sudden disappearance of the cow had infuriated the animal, which was otherwise very quiet and gentle.

That evening I asked Mickey Bawn, our neighbour, if he would oblige me by taking the cow back. Mickey Bawn made light of anything that flew, crawled or swam, and boasted of having power over animals, especially bad-tempered ones. When he returned with the cow walking quietly in front of him, my mother asked, 'Was everything all right, Mickey? Did you get what you wanted?'

'I did, Ma'am,' said Mickey, 'and he did it in great style too.'

Tom 'the bull' kept a book of every service given, and an exact history of the calves obtained from the service of his bull. He would immediately notice any disease or emaciation in an animal and give advice on how it should be treated. He allowed each cow only one service, and was never known to give what the locals called a second 'lep'. He stuck to his belief that the cow was there not for sexual gratification but at Nature's behest, to reproduce. One neighbouring farmer argued that he should allow two services or more to each cow, to which Tom replied hotly, 'No!! No, man! nonsense! You'd only make a whore of your cow.'

Many quaint expressions were heard relating to the subject, though they were never meant to be immoral or offensive. 'Is the gentleman at home, Ma'am?' a neighbour would enquire.

'You mean my husband? He is, Johnny. Do you want him for something, Johnny?'

Johnny shrugs his shoulders and shifts uneasily. 'Yerra, not much, Ma'am, only a few stabs of the bull, that's if he's convainient, Ma'am.'

Some unlucky force seemed to have put a jinx on me as far as bulls and cows were concerned. One Sunday morning it was necessary to have a cow serviced urgently because she was coming late in the autumn. On my arrival the master of the house told me to take the cow to the field where the bull was grazing. It had the remains of an old quarry at one end. He then told me to let the cow loose, which I did. The bull wanted to make friends with

Daisy immediately, but she fobbed him off. The farmer then decided on another plan. We would both hold Daisy by the nose and horns against the upright face of the quarry wall. Daisy squirmed, leaned and stampeded by bending and twisting herself, and gave one last mighty rush as she tried to climb the quarry wall, crushing the knuckles of my left hand against the rock face and leaving me with a nasty gash. Cupid was not shooting straight that morning. After receiving first aid for my wound from the farmer's wife, I took the wayward Daisy home.

III
Making and Mending

BUILDING AND THATCHING

The many skills required and used by the people who lived in my locality were handed down from generation to generation. Thus the head of the household would be able to lay thatch properly and repair it as the need might arise. In other crafts such as basket-weaving, people helped each other to improve their skills. Practical methods were used rather than any show of professionalism or theory.

All the houses in Ballinskelligs were thatched cottages when I was young. The neighbours helped cut the thatching material, bring it to the site and fix it on the roof. Many and various were the kinds of thatch used. The ordinary green rush grew in abundance. It was long and glossy, but when it dried it got so brittle that the soft reed broke in very small sections and was therefore not good material for roofing. Several other kinds of reed grew in the neighbourhood – the forked shorter rush grew in marshland, the needle or spiked rush on the wet margins of salt beaches. Another plant called red sedge, which was short and dense, was in scarce supply except on the marshy slope of a mountain or bogland. Blue sedge was an excellent thatch. It grew on the high sand dunes where it could be seen in great blue tufts, nurtured by the gritty salt sand blown from the sea. It was dry and sharp and required an extra sharp scythe when cutting. Oaten straw and rye were used as an inside coat. The great pharaoh bullrush, called *bearrach* in Irish, was strong, tall and bamboo-like, and ideal for thatch, but alas it did not grow plentifully enough in the area.

Neighbours also helped to build and repair. When a new roof was to be erected this was how the work was done. First the couples were put up. These were a kind of angular truss with an x on top which held the roof tree. Then came the cross-supports, called collar braces, and the long side laths. Wall plates were not used in the construction of these dwellings. The scraw or skin of certain dry bogland was used to cover the timber work. It was tough, elastic and felt-like when dried. Great strips three feet wide, sixteen feet long and two inches thick were cut to an exact measurement. The strips were left to dry and when ready were rolled up like bales of felt, then laid on the lathing, finally covering the entire roof. Long-stemmed purple heather was placed over this in overlapping layers with the stems pointing upwards. Over the heather was laid the white oaten straw, bunch after bunch, the joints always broken as in slating. The last coat was of sedge. The process was slow and it required an experienced thatcher to make the roof watertight. Wooden oak pegs were driven into the wall at two-foot intervals, and a stout rope secured to them. This anchor rope was very important. All the slender grass ropes would be attached to it, over the back of the entire house, six inches apart. The last ropes, horizontal binding ropes called *traisníní*, were important in providing protection from the storm. The last operation was the trimming of the eaves, which extended six inches over the wall of the cottage.

The old thatched cottage was comfortable and warm in winter, and cool in the summer heat. On stormy nights you could hear the rafters creaking in the sheer force of the wind. The hurricanes which swept in from the Skelligs caused havoc to those frail houses. My bed was upstairs on the sheeted loft near the chimney-breast, where I slept very comfortably. My father often woke me in the middle of a winter's storm, telling me to hurry down to the kitchen in case the roof was carried away. The great gusts of wind coming from afar sounded like the booming of the ocean waves and left behind them a vacuum-like whistling sound. Working at night tying down hay and oats, with the rushing roar of a hurricane thundering its way across the Kerry coast, I have heard eerie noises that seemed to come from the body of the storm, a shrieking like the squeal of tormented hogs. The old people spoke of such things and attributed them to the supernatural for lack of a better explanation. My dear mother, Mary Cremin, was a very pious and devout person. I see her now like a bishop sprinkling Holy Water on the walls. She often gathered us around her in the height of the wind, and we knelt and answered her Rosary to the Virgin asking her to intercede with Jesus to calm the storm.

During her petition she never forgot to pray for all the neighbours, including those at sea, that God would shield them from harm.

Several stories are told about the night of the big wind in 1839. Few cottages survived the storm. I heard my father say that ours was demolished, the roof completely blown away. My grandfather Timothy Kirby, his wife Mary Fenton and their family had to seek refuge in a nearby hedge until dawn broke.

Dermot Galvin, a journeyman stonemason, poet and neighbour, was born at Sussa in the Parish of Prior. It was he who composed a poem called 'The Spirit' and another called 'The Fairy Horse'. It was a privilege for me to hear them from his lips. I translate here some of 'The Song of the Hurricane', but its real music and depth can be experienced only in the free-flowing rhythm of the Irish original.

I will write me a line to the people of Ireland,
To get a true story of the damage and loss;
The thatched homes were shattered and scattered all over;
The rumble of thunder and lightning's red flash.

Weary and sorrowful sad is my story,
Engulfed in the darkness of Thursday's black night:
Each man tying stout ropes, the children all wailing
The mothers all tearful, tormented with fright.

We will all raise an outcry from Cashel to Boyne,
From Corrane to Lohar and over to Sneem;
East to Killarney, from Kanturk to Blarney,
Calling roofmen and slaters to come to the scene.

The mason and planer, the mixer of plaster,
The hawk and the trowel, every tool to its trade.
High stages are rising to skyline so airy,
With a party of young men to trim and fit slate.

New eave-chutes from Spain will embellish each building;
Cascading to earth water's torrent will bring.
Each steeple and turret will all be adorned
With large gaping salmon, their beaks to the wind.

Every carpenter, slater and glazier so neatly
On both sides of Erin, this land of great lore,
Will have silver in plentiful heaps to reward them,
Each evening disporting in pleasure and sport.

Coins of copper and silver with notes in abundance
Will fill up our pockets to feast and to dance.
The great king of grace in his will sent the big wind
That dark Thursday night to our lovely green land,
Which tore down the castles between the high mountains
And every neat village up to Dublin's great town.

THE BASKET-WEAVER

An old Irish saying goes: 'The loaded basket is the burden of misery: to the devil the bundle!' Country people were well versed in weaving: nobody would be depending on someone else to make himself a *cliabh* or a *birdeóg*. Neighbours learned the art from each other, though of course the man who had the skill to design and make baskets of all shapes and sizes was the exception. Some were very skilful at making fancy wickerwork. I often watched young men from the village gather in my uncle's kitchen at night-time, making baskets to gamble for in a card game. Eight of them would play, and the stakes were threepence each. That was two shillings for the basket, and the man who won it got it for threepence. They would bring with them a four-inch-deep grassy sod, three feet square, into which the standing rods were pushed, at two-and-a-half-inch intervals, while the slender twigs were woven all round.

The basket was the most important vessel in farming. There were hundreds of uses for it: gathering potatoes, carrying manure, seaweed and turf, taking vegetables, eggs and fish to the market on a fair-day. The large basket which was carried on the back had two sides. It was very important that it fitted comfortably between the shoulders and the small of the back, and this was the side for the carrying rope. The other side was semi-circular. Large square pannier-baskets called *úmacha* were made with hinged bottoms which could be dropped to release the contents. Pairs of panniers were used on the backs of horses or donkeys, supported by a stout pad of matted woven straw. Lobster pots were also woven from green osiers and sally branches.

The biggest basket of all was called a *ciseán*. It was round and bulky and could contain one hundredweight of grain or potatoes. The half basket was next in line, then the *purdy* or little basket. A buxom woman who would be extra broad in the beam would be described as having a *ciseán* of an arse on her.

The man who had learned the art and was expert in weaving was called the *caoladóir*. He had various designs, such as the *birdeóg*, which had the shape of a *naomhóg*. One end of it was pointed and the other square like a boat transom, and it was used specially for filling sacks. Another basket was completely circular, only eighteen inches high, and with lifting loops woven into the top binding. This was used to measure grain and other commodities. A much smaller basket was called the skiff. It was about ten inches across the middle, two feet long and seven inches deep, tapered to a point at both ends, and had arched handles across the top. The skiff was made in a special way: the sally twigs were boiled to remove all skin and sap and give it a creamy white colour. A well-made skiff was a lovely vessel. The housewives would go to market with skiffs under their arms to carry home their purchases. I also saw a child's cradle made from sallies, complete with canopy and rocking blocks.

At one time there was an osier-plot beside every house. When cultivated, the green osier grew long and tall. It was the most important material used for basket-making. Several species of black sally grew wild and were used for weaving the undersides of lobster pots. The twigs and rods were always cut in the dark moon period when the leaves were all gone, and after a few nights' frost had toughened the stems. Osiers cut in the full moon were found to be brittle and less pliable for weaving.

THE COOPER

An old poem about the cooper has a funny twist to it:

What a fool the cooper was
Who hooped his mother
Instead of the cask.

   This rhyme I heard as a child, and to this day I cannot understand it fully. Two coopers worked in Ballinskelligs in my youthful
days: Seán Jerh Moran, from Boolikeel and Thomas O'Connell
from Kinard, both professional coopers who were excellent at
their trade. Wooden casks, tubs, keelers, milk vats, firkins, half-
firkins, buckets, churns: all these wooden vessels were in great
demand. Big wooden tubs were made for storing the milk before
churning. They had wide mouths to give air to the milk and they
were usually placed on wooden trestles a few inches off the ground
so that the air could circulate underneath. A story is told about a
dairymaid who fell into a tub full of cream and was rescued by
the farmer, who said, 'How did you like your swim, Mary?' Mary
was not found wanting in her quick and witty reply: 'It was
alright, Sir, but I had a greasy passage.'
   All the wooden staves were cut and shaped by the cooper. The
best wood for the purpose was hard, black oak called *braicín*. The
grain of this dark oak ran free without knots and it was easy to
split. The cooper would first make rough staves, which he then
fashioned, each stave bow-like on the outside and concave inside.
This gave the belly-shape to the centre of the cask or churn. The
work was done with the cooper's adze, a tool with a curved steel
blade set at right angles to a wooden handle. It was so sharp that
one slip or careless swing could cause a bad accident, but it was
fascinating to watch the cooper using it. How deftly he made the
chips fly! Each swinging stroke had a meaning of its own: light,
medium and deep, they succeeded each other until the piece of
oak had taken a shape pleasing to the eye of the master.

THE BLACKSMITH

The village blacksmith is a hero in folklore not alone in Ireland but in most European countries as well. Tributes are paid to him in song and in story. The blacksmith can make music on his anvil with the hammer, *ding, dong, dédoró ding, dong, déró*. The old saying has it about sharp eyesight:

> *The eye of the hound upon the mountain,*
> *The eye of the hawk above the moor,*
> *The eye of the blacksmith on the nail,*
> *The eye of the maiden at the country dance.*

When shoeing a horse, the smith had to be careful not to touch the quick with the nail, because this would result in the horse becoming lame. In my young days two forges close to Ballinskelligs had enough work between them to employ a pair of blacksmiths with helpers. On certain days the forge filled with people from the locality, each with something to make or to mend. The farm horse stood beside the little cob, the pony and the large draught horses. Mules and donkeys were also kept well shod. The law was very strict on working unshod animals. Some horses had to have a special mouthpiece to quieten them while the blacksmith did his work. Of course mules were most unhelpful and unpredictable, often pointing their rear hooves to heaven.

The smith was usually a mighty man with whiskers on his hands, muscular and unafraid, and possessing a way with animals. He was able to correct the growth of crooked hooves, cure dry decay and let pus from wounds. He treated sprained fetlocks, cured diseased gums and pulled bad teeth. The rough growth which sometimes appeared on horses' gums he cauterized with a white piece of heated steel, before it affected the animal's digestion. Today we have modern cures, but alas horses have become rare in the farming community and are now regarded as the playthings of the rich. The smith had to be competent in making the tools of his trade. He could fashion all the farm implements, the garden spade, the shovel, the *sleán*, and the turf and hay forks. Some blacksmiths were better than others at making and designing farm and household equipment. The smith fashioned the tongs, the pot hooks, the crane, the crook, the three-legged stand, the griddle for home baking. From the forge too came the hinges for hanging the door and the clasp for closing it. The great sickle for seaweed cutting and the little sickle for reaping the harvest were all a product of the blacksmith's skill. He was able to fuse two pieces of iron into a weld, and temper chisels, hatchets and pickaxe points. The ploughshare with its knife and nose and hitching equipment, the loops and shoes for the swinging bar, the open loops and the great circular loop, all these and more he hammered into shape; he made the tools for the slater – the rippers and slate-trimming knives with punch attached, and slate-nails by the thousand. Whenever an army marched or a navy sailed it was imperative that a blacksmith be at hand.

Near Ballinskelligs there once lived a blacksmith called Jamesie Fenton, and his forge stood by the stream of the waterfall in Canuig. He was an old-timer and was a relative of my grandmother Mary Fenton: it is two hundred or more years since his anvil sang. A story is told about a man from beyond the hill in the next townland, who died suddenly while coming back from the market in Cahersiveen. Fortunately he had given a lift on his cart to a woman from Ballinskelligs. It was she who was left with the sad task of guiding the horse homewards with the dead man's body beside her. Some weeks later Jamesie Fenton noticed that the dead man's horse would arrive barebacked and stand near the forge entrance. This became a common occurrence, and the blacksmith seemed unable to send the horse away. One day he noticed that its hooves were in a neglected state, so he took pity on the animal and made it a complete set of new shoes. After giving the horse its freedom the blacksmith watched it gallop across the hill, happy to think he had cared for the horse who had lost its master. Next day he learned that the horse had died suddenly. The old folk attached a superstitious meaning to its death, not understanding that it was only coincidental.

*   *   *

I spent some time working on the New York, New Haven and Hartford railroad in the United States during the thirties. One day I was on the main line between New York and Boston, replacing worn and loose bolts with an Italian from the Tyrol. Having completed the job we were left with some spare time on our hands, and my companion asked me if I could tell him an old folk-tale from Ireland, one about ghosts or the nether world. He was a big kindly man, who showed great interest in the past and in the culture of his native Italy which he had left while yet a youth. I could sense that he was bursting to tell his own story. Traditionally, pride of place in storytelling is given to the older man. I explained that, being the elder, he had the honour of telling the first tale. To my astonishment he started with the Italian folk-tale of Séadhna, word for word as I had heard it in Irish long years before. At one point in the story, the blacksmith put the devil in the leather bag, laid him across the anvil and began to pound the guts out of him with the big sledge-hammer until the devil could stand it no longer and exploded in a blue flash of flame, taking part of the forge roof with him. When John was telling this part of the story, there were tears of enjoyment in his eyes, and his great frame shook with laughter. I didn't have the heart to admit I had heard the story in my native land.

My Italian workmate was a man with a big heart and a hearty laugh: I felt better for having known him. I told him my own story about a blacksmith, nicknamed 'Tim of the Sparks' who was also the local dentist. He would tie one end of a string to the tooth and the other end to the anvil, then push a brand of flaming steel dangerously close to the face. The resulting jerk backwards of the head to avoid the burning steel meant that the tooth was always found hanging to the anvil. One day it is said Tim extracted a good tooth which grew beside an offending one. When the patient protested, Tim had a ready reply: 'I'm only preparing for the extraction.'

Blacksmiths had an old custom of making pocket knives as gifts for their customers. Seán Brúnach, a poet who lived in Top Street, Cahersiveen, two hundred years ago, composed a poem in honour of the knife, praising the perfection of the gift. This is my translation of a stanza from the poem he composed in Irish:

It was fashioned from cast steel
Both burnished and bright;
From the shaft to the point
It would sparkle with light;
The bright smith who drew
On his anvil the blade,
Would share them as gifts
With the good friends he made.

No longer can a horse, mule or pony be seen hitched to the forge wall. We do not need the tongs, the pot hooks or hanging crook any more. The village smithy is closed for ever. No longer can the bell-like music of the hammer on the anvil, *ding, dong, déderó, ding, dong, déró*, be heard to drift on the morning air.

TAILORS

Only a few years ago five tailors found work in the vicinity of Ballinskelligs. The people were not excited about fashion then as they are today: they only wanted the garment to be roomy and comfortable. Certain modes of fashion were seen in the clothes of the well off – the landed gentry, the legal profession, the doctors, the business people and of course the clergy – but they were outside the choice or scope of the ordinary people.

One garment worn by the better classes was the swallowtail coat. It was tight-fitting at the waist and wide to the knee, and the centre panel was the narrow tail hanging from a half-belt at the back. It had two large ivory or black buttons, one on each side of where the tail started. The buttons were nicknamed 'brookers'. The coat was usually worn with a colourful vest with ivory buttons (which were cheap and plentiful) and knee breeches, white stockings, black patent leather shoes, silk scarf and top hat. The gentry of the period also wore great cloaks lined with silk, and half-cloaks. The country people wore a frieze waistcoat without a collar. Some of their *cótaí móra* or greatcoats also lacked collars, perhaps to save the precious homespun material. Trousers were long and wide with slanting pockets called old men's pockets. The horizontal front opening was called the sailor's fly, or the 'ready come out'. When the buttons were opened, the flap would fall down, so it was also called the half-door.

Tailors were known to be witty and well able to tell a story. They were the journeymen 'knights of the needle' who travelled from village to village. Where work was available they would remain as long as they were needed. Mostly unmarried men were those tailors, and because of their fun-loving characters they often became entangled in the nets of the opposite sex. A well-known Irish song has a line which goes, 'My wife has gone with the merry tailor.'

The sewing-machine gradually put finish to the journeyman tailor. Calico and frieze disappeared as time went by. Fashions became more innovative and glamorous. A new, more colourful and lighter material called woollen serge was imported, and very soon suits of serge were to be seen on the people, with perhaps a bowler hat.

A superstition which was kept alive until the late twenties held that the suit belonging to a deceased person should be worn in church for three consecutive Sundays. Sometimes you would see a boy dressed in his father's suit, complete with hard hat, the trousers and jacket too long or too short, as the case might be. The poor Christian often looked ridiculously like a showman. I sometimes feared that if my dear father passed on the same would happen to me, for the thought of looking like the famous Charlie Chaplin in my Dad's suit and bowler hat was too much for me. But thank God the parish priest became aware of the custom and put an end to it.

I do not have much knowledge about women's fashion. Black woollen shawls were worn by young girls and older women. Long wide skirts which swept the floor covered red flannel petticoats. There was no danger you could see the calves or knees of a young girl – you might by chance glimpse the big toes of a bare-footed woman. The black woollen shawl came in very useful for courting couples: if a girl had a sweetheart on the sly, the shawl gave shelter and shade to the young man. I remember how the parish priest condemned company-keeping as immoral. He was known to venture out at night on an odd foray along the byways, armed with a stout blackthorn stick. The following is a translation from the Irish of my poem 'Coinne' or 'Tryst'. It describes the maiden anxiously awaiting her lover for the first time in the secrecy of a country lane.

The old lane is sultry.
I am excited
In expectation,
My breasts on fire
Taut in manacles
Of love.
What matter
If I tread
The withered
Cow turds
That give birth
To green fertility?

Speckled cows
Lie beside the hedge,
Udders swollen
With yellow cream,
Belching and sighing
Chewing and turning
The cud.
Berry-bearing
Briars
Intertwine with
Golden-blossomed
Furze.

Suddenly he stands
Beside me,
Gazing in wonder
At the silver wheel
Of the night.

TAILORS

Instead of stars
In his eyes
I see
Timidity of innocence
Or fear
Of womanhood.

This our first
Meeting,
Concealed,
Forbidden,
Secret.
In the garden
Of desire
Moon shafts
Played
And laid
A silver spell
Of love.

I wove for him
A charm
Of pouted lips.
He glanced
At last
With longing
In his eyes
And with my fingertips
I graved
A silver wreath
Of moonbeams
On his brow.

Hush! Listen! it is
The old priest
Who walks alone
The back road,
And like a wooden bell,

The tapping
Of his thorn stick
Proclaims the night
As if to say,
'Enjoy the light,
Darkness is only
For the groping.'

The speckled cows
Lie comfortable
Beside the hedge,
Sighing and belching,
Chewing and turning
The cud.

The old lane
Is sultry.
Flaming fragrant
Furze blossom
Makes incense
With berry-bearing
Briar.

The old priest
Sleeps.
The wooden bell
Is silent.

I heard my mother talk of women tailors who were called mantle-makers. The mantle was a special garment: a loose cloak with a cape or hood which had frills around the edge to encircle the face. This fashion did not prevail in Iveragh but was worn on the south-eastern seaboard. Reference is made in a traditional song called 'Eochaill', or 'Youghal' to the cloak and the high caul cap:

One Sunday morning into Youghal walking
I met a fair maid upon the way.
Her voice was soft as the fairy music,
Her soft cheeks blushing like dawn of day.

I laid a hand upon her bosom,
I asked a kiss but she answered, 'No,
Kind Sir, be gentle,
Do not tear my mantle,
For none in Erin my grief can know.'

Hoops, lace, light cotton and silk fabric came in with Victoria. I remember a story told more than thirty years ago by an old man who had served as coachman to the local landlord. One day while driving a coach-and-four on a sightseeing tour around by St Finan's Bay near Ballinskelligs, he had six lady passengers wearing wide crinoline dresses with large hoops like billowing balloons. The weather suddenly changed and there was a fearful storm. At a narrow bend on the road the horses could not negotiate the very sharp turn. As the old coachman related it: 'We had to unbuckle the horses and with the help of the ladies and a passer-by we managed to pull the empty coach into the clear. It was the will of God that the ladies weren't carried up into the sky by that gale. The great gusts of wind got under their hoops and blew them inside out, silk was torn, hoops broken, beautiful hats blown away. Whenever the ladies attempted to walk they always ended in the embarrassing position of bottoms up. We had a hard job to get the horses into the shafts of the coach again. The road into Ballinskelligs was more sheltered, and we rested a while at a roadside tavern with a hot drink, before resuming our journey to the big house.' Bamboo and crinoline, however fashionable for the upper class, were not suitable wear for stormy weather on the beautiful but windswept road of St Finan's Bay.

My sister, Mary Kirby, became a seamstress and earned her living in Ireland and in the United States. During her apprenticeship the first thing she was taught was how to make buttonholes. The teacher inspected the work at intervals, and while looking at a sample of Mary's work exclaimed in front of the class, 'Mary, my girl, you'll have to do better! I often saw a better buttonhole under a pig's tail.' Later on, Mary became very successful at her trade, designing and making ballgowns for wealthy people in the United States.

I grieve to think that the era of the village tailor is past. Computers, not people, are in charge of tailoring now. One more landmark, the tailor's shop, has disappeared for ever from country life. If our grandmothers could only see a modern girl going to church on a Sabbath morning dressed in her mini, smelling salts or medical aid would surely need to be administered. I believe that air, water and sunshine are necessary for a healthy body, and that the soul does not need clothing or fashion. In the last analysis grace is the clothing of the soul. Are naked people banned from heaven? As the old man said, blind people are a great pity.

> *The long loose stitch for the fool*
> *The short stitch for the wise.*

THE VILLAGE COBBLER

The shoemaker, too, is gone from the countryside around Ballinskelligs. Only a short while ago the cobbler was a very busy man. At least ten shoemakers worked in our parish before and after the 1914 war. An old rhyme has it as follows:

> *Find four cobblers who can't tell lies,*
> *Find four Frenchmen who are not sallow,*
> *Find four Churchmen who do not covet,*
> *In this Island they are not found.*

The lying shoemaker has vanished, Frenchmen are yellow-skinned as ever. Clergymen are no more covetous than lay people: an old saying goes, 'Monks can't survive on vespers alone.' But the era of the bristle tip, the waxed thread and awl, the iron last and lapstone is no more.

The village cobbler was a most interesting person. People came to him at all times of day and late the night. Sometimes he would teach a young apprentice – perhaps the son of a neighbour – how to fix patches on torn uppers and to sew neatly with the bristled waxed thread. He knew all the local gossip: people confided in him, while coming with their many foot complaints, their corns, bunions and ingrowing toenails. Some cobblers were known to make tight-fitting shoes. One old man swore that the shoes the cobbler made for him would put corns on the hooves of a donkey. The shoemaker sold leather thongs which he cut neatly from the tanned hide, leather belts and leather muzzles for dogs who were known to attack people. I found great pleasure in visiting the cobbler's shop. He was always asking questions which to my mind were amusing and harmless: 'Does your mother keep hens?' 'Are they laying well?' 'Did the cow calve?' 'What colour is the calf?' 'What bull did she get?' 'Are you finished school yet?'

I remember a pair of boots being made for me: size 10, they weighed ten pounds each and were hand-sewn, copper-nailed and wooden-pegged. The soles, three-quarters of an inch thick, were covered with metal hobnails, and the heels were raised with heavy iron tips. They were watertight, warm and durable, and their total cost in 1935 was thirty shillings.

IV
The Living Voice

OUR HOUSE

During the long winter nights, it was good to sit around the open hearth in the warmth of a blazing turf fire. Our house had an open fireplace and chimney-back with built-in stone hob seats on each side. The front wall of the chimney-breast was supported by a great wooden beam which my father said came in on the tide just in time for the building of the house. No matter where the wind blew from, our open chimney never smoked. Our kitchen was lime-washed, and even the walls near the fire were as white as snow every day of the year. Sometimes a change in the weather would bring a lump of soot down from the chimney, to be pounced upon by my watchful mother.

We were all proud of our thatched cottage. There were two bedrooms with a kitchen in between, and space for another bed in the half-loft reached by a ladder. A division of painted boarding separated the kitchen from the bedrooms. The kitchen had a dresser hung with row after row of ware, sometimes in white with a blue and gold pattern. I remember the beautiful china jugs with floral designs which were once full of delicious-tasting red fruity jam. Country people always bought 'the jam in the jug' in preference to the jam in the plain pottery crock. The container helped to adorn the country dresser, and woe betide any slovenly butter-fingers who would break or damage a piece of the precious collection! The kitchen walls were decorated with a picture of Christ and the Virgin Mary, and a piece of Blessed Palm after each Palm Sunday.

A great wicker basket was kept full of turf in its corner at the far end of the kitchen. The fire, continually fed with pieces of pine bogdeal, stayed in until bedtime. It made a lovely blaze and gave off a fragrant smoke. My father dug for these roots, which were found deep in the bogs. The wood, preserved for two thousand years or more, was resinous and inflammable. It was once used for interior lighting, but now made a fine torchlight for spearing fish on rivers, as well as the traditional yule-log at Christmas. Each night a bucket of spring water was brought in for the next morning's breakfast and for drinking. I never drank water more pure and invigorating than the blue crystal from the Bog of the Hummocks. Even in summer it was as cold as ice.

A large wooden peg driven into the wall high up in the corner of the chimney, well out of view, held a supply of salted cod. After about a week the fish would be stiff and dry and flavoured with turf smoke, which gave it a sweet taste. We always ate the smoked cod on Christmas Eve, with a white sauce my mother made from flour, milk and onions and other finely chopped vegetables. During my youth we did not eat much meat except on feast-days. Pork was cheap and plentiful, and pigs' feet were a penny each, but that penny was hard to come by. A pig's head and a large pot of cabbage, turnips and potatoes, washed down by a flood of fresh buttermilk, seemed like food for a king. On the other hand we were lucky in having the choicest of fish, both cured and fresh: nourishing casks of pickled herring with the full roe left in, not to mention mackerel, cod, bream, whiting and other varieties. Our diet varied from time to time as we took advantage of the great tides which exposed the clams, razor clams, scallop and cockles, which we would dig by the bucketful. My mother boiled, cleaned and minced a selection of these mixed with herbs, salt and pepper. This was a mouth-watering clam chowder. The old skinflint with one leg in the grave who drank a cupful of this savoury potion would feel like living again.

All the neighbours kept flocks of geese and had roast and stuffed goose for Christmas and Easter. A goose market was held in Cahersiveen before Christmas. One shilling and sixpence was a good price for a fat goose, while a five-week-old piglet sold for four shillings – a fortune in those days. My mother kept up to forty small yellow hens of an old breed called Sicily Buí, as well as small black hens with a few speckled feathers on the wings, called Black Minorca, before Rhode Island Reds were introduced to Ballinskelligs. We also kept a dozen or more ducks with a great mallard-like drake. Eggs were plentiful and cheap when all the hens were laying, and fetched thirty-six or forty pence for one hundred and twenty. The cock rarely announces daybreak in the countryside now. As one old-timer put it, on hearing the cock crow after a sleepless night: '*Tar slán, a mhic na circe!* A health to you, son of the hen!'

My father had seven acres which seemed over-stocked. They fed two milch cows, always of the Black Kerry breed, and two calves which were sold as yearlings. We kept a donkey and cart, with a creel to bring home the turf. Every inch of those seven acres had to be utilized, to grow potatoes, oats, and hay for winter fodder. The cattle and the donkey were left with little room for grazing. The annual rent on the seven acres was three pounds ten shillings, payable to the Mary O'Mahony Estate of Dromore, and later to the Irish Land Commission, until the parcel of land was finally redeemed by the occupying tenant.

Ballinskelligs and the surrounding countryside of Iveragh was vested in the O'Mahony and Fitzgerald families. Other parts were owned by Trinity College, Dublin, and by the Marquis of Lansdowne. Landlords did not have a good name. If a tenant was unable to pay his rent he slept by the roadside. An old widow was evicted from a little cabin whose ruins are still visible on the roadside near Canuig, Ballinskelligs. As the sheriff and bailiffs threw her from her miserable holding, the widow cursed in Irish, 'May a funeral of demons escort your soul to Hell!' Some of my neighbours suffered a similar fate. A platoon of Redcoats with guns and fixed bayonets travelled from Tralee to Ballinskelligs, where they wreaked vengeance on the O'Leary family, who were in arrears to the Crown to the sum of a few paltry shillings. Denis O'Leary, his daughter Brigid and three sons resisted with pitchforks, and it was only on the intervention of the parish priest that the old man's life was spared. Because the Chief Constable was injured in the fray, old Denis was put in irons and taken fifty miles to Tralee, bound like some wild animal, bruised and broken in both soul and body.

The land of Ballinskelligs was divided into small uneconomic holdings, and the region was registered with the Congested Districts' Board. In the entire parish perhaps only ten people would own enough land to farm twenty cows and keep a pair of horses. These 'strong' farmers, who cultivated an air of independence and pride, were sometimes referred to as 'squireens'. A great social barrier existed between them and the poor men or women struggling to survive on à few acres.

THE JOURNEYWORKERS

My thoughts go back once more to the long winter nights of my early boyhood – the floor swept clean, Mom putting an apronful of black turf from Gob an Dá Chaol into the fire, the day's work finished till tomorrow. After supper the neighbours would visit each other, a custom called cabin hunting, night rambling and other such terms in Irish. It gave neighbours a chance to relax from the tensions of their daily lives and chat about topical affairs.

I remember Tomáisín, a regular caller to our house, as an old man of nearly eighty. Although he attended only a hedge school, he was able to read and write, do mental arithmetic and discuss things. He preferred the clay pipe to the wooden one, and he would often ask my mother for the loan of a knitting needle to free the stem. My mother hated the smell of tobacco, and when she would see the men rubbing the knitting needle on their trousers afterwards, she would say to them in Irish, 'You are a bloody dirty lot!'

Another neighbour who often came was Andy Gow O'Sullivan. Andy was an old man when I got to know him. He owned a thatched cabin about fifty paces west of our house. The land he had would not make a graveyard for a wren – it consisted only of the pathway to his door. He was one of the journeymen workers called the *spailpíní fánacha*. The tools of their trade were the spade, shovel and reaping sickle. I have often heard Andy telling stories about the great harvest and grain reaped by the special harvest *meitheal* or work party, and about the skilled use of the reaping sickle and the implements for preparing potato and vegetable beds. The journeymen of the past were specialists in their own way. Their work was neat and produced an excellent crop yield.

Seasonal migration from Ballinskelligs became traditional after the Famine. Workers travelled on foot to Tralee, their spades on their shoulders as a sign of their trade. If they got no work there, they would continue their walk, to the markets in Limerick city or Tipperary town. After a hard journey, in poor clothes and bad shoes and with little to eat, these fine workers were easily hired at a low wage by the rich farmers.

Andy would describe the beautiful country mansions owned by big farmers and also told tales of the horsy people who owned packs of hounds for fox hunting. According to him, any worker hired to become a hand at the Big House would consider himself fortunate. Whenever Andy became slightly inebriated he would talk about the beautiful women who made up his youthful love life. Without a doubt he would have been a dashing young blade: he was yet tall and handsome even in the evening of his days.

While I write about the travelling work parties, it is only just and right that I fill the page with knowledge of the past that my dear mother handed down to me. My mother Mary Cremin and Eileen Connell of Dungeagan travelled to County Limerick in the year 1877. They left Ballinskelligs with another group in the late spring of that year, walking most of the long journey, and they worked for nine months before returning home barefoot in deep snow. My mother was only eighteen, and Nelly O'Connell one year her senior. They were fortunate in meeting with good people who hired both of them at the market-place in Limerick city: rich farmers owning acres broad and free which were used mostly for dairying. The girls were put in company with other girls, under the management of a stewardess, and stayed in a special house near the dairy. It was a hard life, constantly milking evening and morning. The milking started at five o'clock. Afterwards the great churns were set up for the hand churning, which was heavy work. There was other work too: food had to be prepared for pigs, potatoes harvested, washing and ironing done. My mother said she often felt so exhausted going to her bed that it was terrible to think of another day's work starting at the dawn. Sunday was no different from any other day: there was no day of rest. They only wore their shoes going to Mass, because they had to last for a year at least. Their entire wages for nine months were eight pounds. This was the grim story my mother told about the life of the seasonal workers.

Many fine young men who went over the hills with their spades were never to return. Some were hired by unscrupulous farmers and had to sleep in cold lofts over the stables, where they contracted illnesses and died as a result. Many others joined the army: they wanted to be freed forever from the misery of the journeyworker's life and they did not care that it was a change from the house of Horror to the house of Hate. There was little choice between being a private in the king's army and being a beggar and a journeyman. An Irish poem called 'An Spailpín Fánach' or 'The Journeyworker' is sung to a haunting air. A translation of its first verse will give an idea of its richness:

Never never more shall I go to Cashel,
Selling or wasting my manhood
At the market-place
By the hiring wall,
Like a pauper on the sidewalk.
Churlish landlords
Arriving on steeds,
Inquiring if I am for hiring,
Oh come let us go,
For the road is long,
Come away with the Spailpín Fánach.

GHOSTS

A lovely beach about a mile long stretches west from Bearna Dhearg, the Red Gap, to the old ruined castle at Ballinskelligs. On moonlit nights when the tide was low, the Ghostly Rider of the Red Gap sent an eerie sound echoing through the harbour by the dint of his running. Who was this invisible Rider of the Red Gap?

The old people told of him by their firesides, about when Paddy Thomas was collecting planks of driftwood on the beach at Ballinskelligs and the Ghostly Rider rode furiously by him on the wings of the wind. It put an end to Paddy's beachcombing that night at any rate. And as he said later on, 'That was bad enough, but to leave my jacket, my pipe and my tobacco after me on the sand. He ran like a greyhound, the bastard!'

Daniel Cremin went about his business without paying much heed to talk about ghosts or the supernatural. He was collecting sea kelp one night to manure his potato garden for the coming spring. It was as bright as day under the brilliant moonlight.

I was the only man who was collecting the broken kelp that night, with no one below me, or abreast of me. I was working easily, without hurry or urgency. The beach was covered with great heaps of the broken sea wrack left after the receding tide. I had the mule with two big pannier baskets slung across the thick straw straddle on its back.

'It was only a matter of filling the baskets and emptying them above high-water mark, making a great heap of the kelp on high ground to be drawn home on the farm cart later on. I had filled a load on the baskets, when the mule suddenly took fright and fled, and before I had time to grasp the rein the creature was labouring under its load of sea kelp half-way up the steep strand. You could hear blasts of superfluous gas exploding from the animal's rear end, as it struggled and strained its way up through the soft sand.

'Very soon after, I heard in the distance the sound of a horse's hooves beating loud on the sand, the lash of the whip, the creaking of saddle leather, and the laboured breathing and snorting of a horse at its utmost speed. It swept by me like a squall of wind, sending great showers of broken kelp into the sky, as a swooping hawk scatters the smaller birds. I am not easily startled, but this time I made the Sign of the Cross and started for home a mile away to Ballinskelligs West. There I found the mule awaiting me, cropping the grass in the field near the house, and still carrying the kelp. When I removed the load and harness from its back, the creature was bathed in sweat. I put it into the stable, and gave it some water and clean hay.'

This was the story of Daniel Cremin about one hundred and twenty years ago.

As for myself, I have often walked the sands of the beach at the full of the moon and in darkness too, in the dead of night, but all

I ever heard or saw was the eternal lullaby of the ocean as the little waves lapped, one after another, forever and forever more. My farewell to you, Ghostly Rider of the Red Gap, or perhaps of the imagination!

*   *   *

Tales of the White Spirit of Béal na Méine, the Mouth of the Maine, were common throughout Munster. This was an apparition in the form of a dazzling white light. Tradition tells of a she-devil who caused the death of two people. The apparition is supposed to have appeared on the Ring of Kerry road, near the village of Sneem. Our next-door neighbour, Michael Curran, stayed up on three consecutive nights with a cow he expected to calve. He came into my father's kitchen, and my father asked if his cow had given birth.

'Yes,' said Michael, 'a calf was born this morning.'

'What kind of calf did she have?' asked my father.

'Yerra!' said Michael, 'the calf is as white as the spirit of the Maine.'

Other tales told of different apparitions. The *púca*, a dark, misshapen spirit was a bad omen for the person who would meet or see it. Another, a black dog, was supposed to be the devil in an assumed shape. The evil spirit took many forms: a beautiful woman, and very often a pig or swine. There was a place on the road to Kilreelig where horses were known to bolt night or day. This place was called Pluais na bPreab, the Turn of the Starts. The jarvey usually took the horse by the head, leading it by in safety. Old people believed the two most sensitive animals in this respect to be the thoroughbred horse and the greyhound.

Cnocán na mBuachaillí, the Hillock of the Boys, was on the beach-front, west of the Garda Station at Ballinskelligs. Local folklore tells how many people had heard the noise and excitement of a hard-fought hurling game, with ghostly hurling teams and their spiritual supporters, the clash of the ash, the cheering after scores and all the unseen clamour which told of opposing teams in deadly competition. Some actually swore to having seen the *buachaillí* at play. This was not confined to Ballinskelligs. All over the country, in fields, on beaches and in valleys, the fairy hosts were supposed to play their many games. In one such other field at Cnocán na hUaighe, the Hillock of the Grave, near Dungeagan, Ballinskelligs, the ghostly athletes were wont to play in the full of the moon, and the excitement of the game was often heard from afar. My father's fishing seine net was always spread out on the Hill of the Boys. Superstitious people said this should not be done, just in case the good people decided they would like to use the pitch. However, it seemed the Boys had no objection to my father's seine net: it was the most successful in the harbour.

A little bridge spans the stream called Ballinskelligs River on the road to Bolus. At this bridge in the eighteenth century it is said that another ghostly spirit took up residence. The spirit in this case was a washerwoman constantly bittling clothes on a flat rock near the bridge. I heard my mother tell how she often heard the noise coming from the rock at the bridge. Several brave people tried to catch up with her, but the noise of the bittling was always the same distance away.

Time has passed and the washerwoman has departed from her vigil at the bridge. The spirit-boys who were so frolicsome have forsaken their games on the hillock by the sea. The big basket of turf is not kept in the kitchen any more to feed the blaze on the hearth, and the neighbours no longer practise storytelling. These customs are now part of the past. My eyes are weary from the glare of colour television. I am a part of an old world being initiated into the new.

SOME POETS AND A STORYTELLER

From 1650 to 1800 poetry and poets flourished in Ireland. Poets were many in Munster alone, often vying with each other, making poetry in beautiful forms. These masters of the language did not speak the ordinary Irish of today. One of their number was Eoghan Rua Ó Súilleabháin (1748-84), who had poetry ever flowing from his lips like a stream in torrent. This is a stanza translated from one of his poems:

Poems to relate and simulating gentle tones,
Dancing and disporting with females untimorous,
Stately maidens swarming by my side in tranquillity,
Silken and happy, pleasant, kindly and chaste.

Eoghan travelled throughout South Kerry, often teaching in hedge schools. He was a vagabond and a spendthrift who had a way with women. Young girls were attracted to him in companionship and pleasure. Undoubtedly he had a mysterious power which was called the *ball seirce* or love charm, and his flattery could win any woman he liked. It is said that he deflowered as many as one hundred and eighty-nine maidens. Be that as it may – he who is without blame, let him cast the first stone. The oldest game on earth, the game on the mossy sward, is still played and will be forever.

In his youth Eoghan was courting a young neighbouring girl. He had been her companion for some time and the girl had fallen in love with him. One summer evening, as the lovers strolled by the river bank, they came to a ford where stepping-stones were placed in the stream to enable people to cross dry-shod. Eoghan and his love were carefully making their way across when she slipped and fell into a deep pool. The water splashed up under her clothes and wet her. On reaching the bank, the story goes, the girl took off her wet clothes, and turning to Eoghan she said, 'Look, Eoghan, the water jumped up on me – the water itself has more nature than you have.' For that occasion the poet composed the fine lullaby 'Seo Leo a Thoil', which I have translated:

All ye bards in disgrace
From Cashel to Doon,
And you of my tribe
Who may grieve for my kind,
Come listen henceforth,
To my teaching give mind,
And see what misfortune
Will always be mine.

And hush a bye,
Do not cry for a while,
Hush my baby,
My treasure and store;
Your eyes are weeping,
And wanting your feed,
Hush my baby,
Do not cry a tear.

When first I met
With this young pretty maid,
Her eyes were green,
And her cheek like the rose;
She did not refuse me
When her I approached:
My grief, I knew not
The trouble in store.

Her troublesome eyes
And scheming also:
A fair one who'd play
The oldest game known;
She left me all loaded
With sorrow and woe,
A-rocking a baby
And weeping alone.

What plans for the future
For a child of this kind?
Not a drop in my organs
For a soft way of life;
Listen, my baby,
Without doubt you will get
All the good things of life
I propose for you yet.

And hush a bye,
Do not cry for a while,
Hush my baby,
My treasure and store;
Your eyes are weeping,
And wanting your feed,
Hush my baby,
Do not cry a tear.

The following story was told far and wide in South Kerry. On one of the many days Eoghan spent there he met a group of schoolchildren. He had reason to believe that since he had sown some of his wild oats in this region several years before, some of the youngsters should show a poetic strain. Rogue that he was, he would put them to the test. So he saluted them. 'Listen a while, boys! Could ye be so kind as to tell me the name of this townland I'm in at present?' All the youths answered with one voice, 'This is the townland of Abhainn an Gharraí, the garden river.'

'Indeed,' said the poet, 'the garden river of the fragrant shrubs!' Not a tree or shrub adorned the place except a potato garden in full bloom beside the road. The poet pointed to this and said, 'That's the garden of the fragrant shrubs, and the boy who will complete the rhyme, I'll give him sixpence.' One boy jumped over the ditch and picked a potato stalk with a cluster of young potatoes clinging to the roots, and holding it up facing the poet, said:

This is the garden river
Of the fragrant shrubs so sweet,
These are the fragrant shrubs
That hold their fruit beneath.

The poet gave the boy the sixpence and told him, 'Whenever we meet again I'll give you the same.' Eoghan went on his way, but he hadn't much of the road behind him before the same boy appeared in front of him with his hand out. 'What do you want?' asked the poet. 'The other sixpence,' said the boy. 'You told me if we ever met again you'd give me another one.' Eoghan had no doubt but that he had a boy as clever as himself to contend with.

Another story is told of how Eoghan fell in love with a young widow with one son. Eoghan was teaching him at the local hedge school. By all accounts the widow had no great time for Eoghan and disdained his advances. She had a beautiful crown of flaxen hair, such as he described in verse:

> Her hair a garland,
> Crozier-like and kinky skeins,
> Like gloss of gold
> Without shadow or haze.

One evening as school was ending the poet called the widow's son aside, telling him to cut a lock of his mother's hair while she was sleeping, and bring it to him the next day. He would use the magic of the *ball seirce* which never failed him: if one lock of a maiden's hair came into his possession she could not but return his affection. What did the boy do but tell his mother the master wanted a lock of her hair. The mother said, 'Well and good, my son. I'll have it ready for you for school tomorrow.'

Now, that widow had a large fierce dog of mongrel breed, with a golden-yellow coat. She cut a shiny yellow tress from the dog's tail, tied it with a silken ribbon and gave it to her son for the poet, along with an invitation for him to come and visit her. Eoghan was delighted. His heart was light with expectation as he neared the widow's house, whistling and singing. Alas! if he had no story coming, he had one going away, for the fierce yellow dog tore the trousers off him, and the poet decided that a good run was better than a bad stand.

Eoghan Rua Ó Súilleabháin stood out among his contemporaries. He wove words in the loom of his mind with never a difficulty, and there was music and rhythm to all he wrote. This gifted poet had no shortage of themes: love, sadness, conviviality, the wrath of war and the tumultuous storm. I feel true humility drinking a sip from the crystal spring of his legacy, and regret not taking more interest in what was said and told: a vast amount of knowledge and story is covered for ever by the great slab and the green sod.

*   *   *

Diarmuid O'Shea was born near Kenmare between 1750 and 1760. He stayed for some time in Ballinskelligs as boatman to Francis Sigerson, sailing and managing a hooker kept in the little harbour there. Diarmuid was a gifted poet, giving voice to verse like the bubbling swirl of a stream.

The parish priest of that area had joined Diarmuid and a local woman in wedlock. All was bliss until some busybody revealed that Diarmuid had a blood relationship with his new wife: this was frowned upon by the Church of the time. The parish priest decided that the marriage was invalid and forbade any further meeting between the couple. Diarmuid reverted to bachelorhood in his little cottage near the shore. The story is told of how his former spouse would stand on the hillock, waving her love to her separated husband. Diarmuid composed a poem which he called 'An Scur', 'The Untying of the Marriage Bond'. In this poem he castigates the parish priest in six stanzas, of which I have translated the second:

> *Oh Mary and Jesus,*
> *Bright King of nature*
> *Without sin,*
> *Who gathered together*
> *In church yard*
> *All my kith and kin;*
> *Who will light the candles,*
> *And lay my bones to rest,*
> *Or who will call the neighbours*
> *When I sink*
> *In the abyss of death?*

A local man was heard lamenting over his brother's corpse in Ballinskelligs in the year of the cholera plague in Europe. People said he was composing poetry unknown to himself:

My grief, my brother,
My curse on death,
Seven cursed be the plague.
Why do you sleep so much?
This world cannot rouse you:
The clamour of the fair,
Nor the army of King James.

In 1785, a year after Eoghan's death, another poet was born in Iveragh. Though an Ó Súilleabháin, and a schoolmaster, Tomás Rua was not related to the great Eoghan. He taught at Caherdaniel, Portmagee, Ballinskelligs and Waterville, and worked as a postman plying the roads between Cahersiveen and Derrynane before dying in 1848.

On one occasion he lost all his books when a hooker grounded on a submerged reef as it left Derrynane harbour. Tomás composed 'Amhrán na Leabhair', 'The Song of the Books', to lament their loss and curse the captain of the hooker, Dermot Rua O'Rahilly, whose people are still living in the townland of Reen, Ballinskelligs. Dermot Rua spent most of his life fishing out of Ballinskelligs Bay and Derrynane harbour. He often sailed his hooker northward beyond Bolus Head and into the Portmagee channel. His sister Ellen O'Rahilly married Jerry Kirby, my great-grandfather, in the year 1814. I heard my father say that Dermot Rua suffered from failing eyesight in latter years and this affected his skill in handling the vessel under sail.

Tomás declares in his poem that he was asked by the authorities of the day to go to Portmagee and teach for some time. He had all his books and teaching material packed into great sacks which he loaded on board Dermot Rua's hooker to be delivered to Portmagee. It was a fair night as the hooker weighed anchor. She was slipping through the treacherous gap of Derrynane harbour when the wind suddenly failed. The hooker lost way and slewed onto a shallow reef where her planking caved in. Dermot Rua was at the helm and in his panic threw all the books overboard. The poor people of the time were superstitious about poets, whom they regarded as cut off from ordinary mortals. They were considered to have the power of good or evil, and those on whom a poet laid his curse would be unlucky for the rest of their lives. When Tomás Rua composed 'The Song of the Books' he cursed Dermot O'Rahilly:

> It was Dermot Rua O'Rahilly
> Who cast the books into the sea:
> May the red demons hoist him
> Away up into the sky.

When Ellen O'Rahilly heard the verse being sung, with a dire curse on her brother, she vowed to wreak vengeance on the poet. The country roads were mere cattle tracks, and Tomás Rua travelled by pony to and from his native Caherdaniel. The road from Portmagee led across a beautiful mountainous district through St Finan's Glen, over the hill of Coom and down into the valley of Ballinskelligs. This was the place where Ellen O'Rahilly Kirby lived. Having observed the poet's movements, she lay in wait for him on a certain evening. The unfortunate Tomás ran into a barrage of rocks and stones, together with a venomous tongue-lashing. He tried to escape but the woman was beside herself with fury. Coming down from his saddle he implored her in God's name to cease hostilities. 'Wait! Wait! be patient, good woman!' said Tomás. 'The poet was full of fury like you are now when he composed that verse, fury and sadness for the loss of his books. When a cask is full, it only spills out what is within.'

Then he raised the curse from Dermot O'Rahilly and transferred it to the rock that caused the disaster:

> God's curse and His Church's
> Be on that hateful horrid rock,
> Which sank the ship
> Without fury of the storm,
> Without a wind or gale!

It was no wonder that the poet suffered great distress, for on that same night that his books were lost, his clothes were also destroyed by fire. Here he mourns their loss:

My sorrow, grief and weariness:
I'm the relic of great misery,
Forever in lamentation
For my own sad case.

My wearing apparel scattered
Which was made and fashioned for me,
And came from out of Banba,
As a flower that I should wear.

My books are gone into the sea,
Which makes the story sad,
And my clothing consumed within the flames,
While I lay in trance-like sleep.

That morning people pitied me
So sorrowful bewailing,
And the cold I felt had chilled me,
Without shelter from the sky.

Tomás Rua was about ten years younger than Daniel O'Connell, who observed the poet's genius, and had him sent to a college in Dublin. There the atmosphere, cold and anglicized, was so different to that of his kindly Iveragh that he never felt happy. At the end of three years, he was sent to hospital by order of the visiting physician, Mr John O'Riordan. He appealed to God of the Universe to bring him safe from the house of disease, in Irish verse later sung as a hymn called 'A Rí an Domhnaigh', 'King of Sunday':

O King of Sunday, with aid come near me,
Bring succour to each aching pain;
Bright King of Monday, be always constant
And from your keeping may I never stray.
O King of Tuesday, with heart so loving,
Be Thou my shield on Judgment Day;

O King of Wednesday, do not let me languish,
In bondage far from my kith and kin.
O King of Thursday, I crave forgiveness,
All Your righteous rules I have breached in sin;
O King of Friday, do not keep reckoning
Of each wilful act and each foolish whim.
O King of Saturday, I ever plead You
To guide me safe beyond Acheron's shore;
May Your sacrifice be my shield and patron
In Paradise for evermore.

Tomás Rua was a close friend of Father Dermot O'Sullivan, scion of the O'Sullivan chieftains of the Béara peninsula in West Cork. According to local lore, he was also an able poet. His presbytery, the White House, was in Kinard West where the O'Connell family now live. This priest was generous, charitable and holy. The poor people of Prior parish called him the Prince because of his work among the sick and destitute who had barely survived the Great Famine, and they loved him so much they would kneel on the open roadway when he approached. It was said that he often healed the sick and had supernatural powers. This rumour spread until it reached the ears of the bishop in Killarney. One day the bishop arrived with two other priests at the presbytery in Kinard West, where they were entertained by Father O'Sullivan to dinner. During the meal, in the ebb and flow of conversation about the Church and other topics, the bishop found an opportunity to mention the rumours. Was it true that the priest had used strange powers of healing? The bishop asked for a drink and Father Dermot filled him a glass of spring water. On taking the glass to his lips the bishop observed that it was a glass of red wine, at which he became amazed and said, 'But Father Dermot! I only asked for a glass of water!'

'Oh yes, Your Lordship!' exclaimed the other. 'See what the glass contains now.' It was clear spring water once again. It is said that the bishop blessed him and, thanking him for his hospitality, went on his way to Killarney.

Father O'Sullivan was also the author of a book on divinity, in which he had a doctorate. Tomás Rua composed a poem of praise to the good priest called 'The Pleasant Prince'. This is a translation of the first verse:

> *He is Doctor of Divinity and Holiness,*
> *The best in cleric coat and deed;*
> *We are all the better*
> *Since he came among us,*
> *And all interested*
> *In his good counsel;*
> *A branch of light,*
> *A servant of Jesus Christ,*
> *A brave and active soldier,*
> *He is Dermot of the bright heart,*
> *He is the Prince I boast of,*
> *The flower of all good chieftains.*

*   *   *

It seems like yesterday that I watched my son hauling lobster pots by the side of the Scéalaí Rock. Scéalaí, storyteller – the word broke like a flash from the shadows on the hillside above us. I looked up at the deserted village of Cill Rialaig, where Seán Ó Conaill was born on 21 March 1853, within view of the Scéalaí Rock, as if Nature herself had prepared a monument at the birthplace of the King of the Storytellers.

Seán's name has become synonymous with Gaelic culture. A professor of Gaelic folklore, Dr James Delargy, was first introduced to him by Fionán MacColum (co-founder of the Gaelic League) in August 1923. Armed only with a small notebook and pencil, Dr Delargy transcribed a wealth of stories from the lips of a great *seanchaí*, and published them in *Leabhar Sheáin Uí Chonaill*. Many of these tales were of local origin, but Seán also told stories about Fionn and the Fianna, the Druids, the Táin, Diarmuid and Gráinne and Cú Chulainn. He was familiar with sagas whose roots were in ancient Greece, tales which seemed to hang between the spirit world and reality. Writers and scholars still marvel at this humble storyteller whose only schooling was two weeks' attendance at the local hedge school.

The voice of my mother tongue seemed to live again in the breeze which came down from the deserted village on the cliff-top to where we hauled our lobster pots. I thank God for Seán's legacy to the Gaeltacht, and for the pride he gave me in my cultural heritage.

THE ISLAND OF THE FAIR WOMEN

Long long ago, Lúd and Seirce lived on a little Island at the mouth of the great estuary of Inbhear Scéine. They were deeply in love. Lúd of the Black Spear was a young man better than men, an otter in water, and a warrior on land. No one knew where Seirce came from. Her hair fell to the ground in shining tresses and the gloss of the sloe fruit shone in every cluster. Her throat was as white as the wild *ceannbhán*. People whispered, shook their heads and said she was not of this world: she was a devil woman, a queen who came from the Island of the Fair Women.

St Patrick had not yet arrived in Ireland, so Christian marriage was not practised. One day while Lúd and Seirce were having fun on the beach, Lúd spoke: 'Seirce! would you like to come and stay with me forever?'

Seirce answered and said, 'I was fearful, Lúd, that you might never speak these words to me. I am ready to come with you at any time.'

'When light breaks the dawn?' said Lúd.

'When light breaks the dawn!' said Seirce.

'With the ebb of the tide?' said Lúd.

'With the ebb of the tide!' said Seirce.

Seirce and Lúd stood on the strand in the speckled light of dawn. They divested their bodies of all clothing. Lúd turned towards the East and Seirce towards the West, and they stayed in this position until the sun rose. Then Lúd knelt and bowed his head three times to the risen sun and Seirce knelt and bowed three times to the ocean. Lúd rose and drew a wide circle with his black spear on the golden sands, drawing a dividing line through the middle of the circle. He stood on the right of the division and Seirce stood on the left, until the waves of the ocean washed all traces of the circle and its division from the sand. They waded into the sea hand in hand, and looking towards the sun gave three great shouts of joy, for they were now joined in wedlock by the waters of the earth and the fire of the sun – the gods they gave homage to before the coming of Patrick.

The signs of nature were right. Ronán the seal rolled over on the flat rock at the harbour's mouth and the dolphins leaped with joy. But Seirce noticed that small dark clouds were appearing over the Island of the Fair Women. When Seirce and Lúd came out of the water, they went to a secluded loop in the woods where they lay under the rays of the sun. There she received with love to her womb Lúd of the Black Spear, the otter and the warrior. From then on they were busily at work building a little house beside the harbour. Seirce wove the wall from wattles and branches of osier which grew wild in the woodland, while Lúd mixed the red clay which he poured into the frames. In a short while the house was ready to live in.

Lúd owned a light canoe, a gift from his father before he was drowned in the great squall of wind from the red moon. The canoe had the tail of a seagull and the breast of a swan. Old fishermen nicknamed it the boat with the bald prow, and it had speed, protection and carrying capacity. The more fearful the high breakers, the more the canoe stood like a water-sprite on the crest of each wave. Seirce collected the wild bog-cotton and the fine fairy flax. Every night she would spin with urgent endeavour, besides helping Lúd to add thousands of new meshes to his nets. By this time Seirce was heavy with child, and there was an urgency to have the little clothes and other necessities for the occasion. Lúd brought large salmon from the narrow lake, so they suffered from neither hunger nor thirst, but were in perpetual love with one another. The pangs of childbirth started, with Seirce foretelling her time was nigh. Lúd went to the shade of the woods, where he prepared a couch of branches and withered grasses, covered with a great deerskin. Seirce came and lay on the bed prepared for her, while Lúd of the Black Spear, the otter and the warrior, stood by her.

'By the incoming tide,' said Lúd.

'By the incoming tide,' said Seirce.

When the tide turned to fill, a beautiful female child came into this life without trouble or pain. The signs of nature were favourable. Ronán the seal rolled over on the flat rock of the harbour, and the dolphins leaped with joy, but Seirce still noticed the dark clouds rising beyond the Island of the Fair Women. Lúd of the Black Spear had woven a cradle from the great bulrushes for his daughter, who had the likeness of a queen on her countenance.

The long days of summer were shortening, and the long nights of harvest were closing in. Lúd had to be early on the mountain and late on the ocean, hunting, fishing and trapping, so that the larder might be filled with the fruits of the earth for the winter days ahead. He often stayed in his canoe until the day broke, cunningly placing the meshes before the fish of the night. Many a long hour did Seirce sit alone, mending the broken meshes of the nets and spinning until the dead hour of night, while little Niavra slept peacefully in her cradle on the hearthstone.

One night as Seirce was peacefully pursuing her work, and Lúd out in the harbour, there was a knock on the door. Thinking it was Lúd who had come in from the sea, she opened the door to welcome him. At that moment six women brushed past her into the kitchen. They were the most beautiful women that Seirce had ever laid eyes on. Their long golden hair fell loosely in loops to the ground, the golden rays of the sun seemed to sparkle from each flaming tress, their eyes shone a bright blue-green and glowed with a piercing light, and each wore a crown resembling deer antlers. Seirce became alarmed and demanded to know who they were and whence they came, but they answered with mocking laughter and words spoken in a language she could not understand. They soon made themselves busy at weaving and mending the nets. Seirce noticed that they were forever casting glances towards the cradle where the child lay sleeping. By this time the night was well advanced. Then the woodcock spoke his clarion cry announcing the light of dawn, and all the women jumped with fear and disappeared through the door like a gust of wind. Seirce, frightened and disturbed by the events of the night, went to the spring for water, and heard a voice speaking to her in the soft morning light:

'Seirce! I am the spirit of your grandfather. Give ear to what I have to say to you. The women who came to you last night were spirits, demon women from the Island of the Fair Women. They are jealous of your child because she will be more beautiful than they are. They will come again tonight to take her and put a changeling in her place. Listen well to my advice. Let them into the house as before, but first make a small wooden cross of twigs and hide it in the child's cradle. This cross will be the symbol of a man who will come to Ireland, and it will have power over evil spirits. Do not mention these things to Lúd in case he will not go hunting or fishing any more. When the women are busily weaving or mending the nets go to the doorway, and on looking out into the night exclaim in a frightened voice: "Look, look, the Island of the Fair Women is being consumed in flames!"'

Night came, and so did the six demon women. They immediately set to work, busily weaving and mending the nets, but Seirce noticed they were whispering and laughing among themselves. After some time had passed Seirce went to the door, where she stood for a long time looking out into the night. Suddenly, wild-eyed and screaming, she exclaimed, 'The Island of the Fair Women is being consumed by flames!' The demon women started to scream and shout in one voice, 'My house and my children! My house and my children!' while they also attempted to snatch the baby from the cradle. But a light in the form of a cross surrounded the cradle, and scattered the demon women like the leaves of autumn. Lúd came with the break of dawn, his little boat lying low in the water with the fruits of the sea. He laid his spear near the cradle of the child and kissed her thrice.

Then Lúd and Seirce went together to the golden sands and, turning together towards the rising sun, they uttered three shouts of joy. They lived happy and contented forever after. All the signs were favourable. Ronán the seal rolled over on the harbour stone, the dolphins leaped with joy, and Seirce noticed that the sky was no longer dark beyond and above the Island of the Fair Women.

It was my mother who told this old folk-tale to me. If it is a lie, so be it, for I am neither the creator nor the composer.

AN ELIZABETHAN TALE

The Strand of the Englishman is an extension of Rinn Rua, the Red Reef. This lovely beach lies under the townlands of Emlagh and Fermoyle. A stout ship under the command of Sir Edward Denny sailed into Ballinskelligs Bay during the reign of Queen Elizabeth. The ship's larder was in need of victuals, for Sir Edward was returning to England after a long sea voyage. He cast anchor a quarter of a mile east of Rinn Rua, where he ordered a boat ashore, carrying twenty armed seamen with swords and muskets. Their leader served notice on the people, demanding that a herd of fat bullocks together with all the other victuals needed to replenish the ships' stores be delivered on the beach at the end of three days. A public order proclaimed that severe reprisals would ensue if the locals disobeyed a servant of the Crown. The Knight then took a man on board, to be held as hostage until the order was fully complied with. Sir Edward was given assurances that the stores would be available on the beach on the day appointed. The people collected the cattle and all other requirements and placed them within sight of the ship on a small green field near the sandy beach, leaving a few men to be seen guarding the victuals. The remainder positioned themselves amongst the sand dunes and behind hedges and dykes near the fields under cover of darkness, crudely armed with pitchforks and weapons of every sort. The English came ashore with twenty marines armed with cutlasses and muzzle-loading muskets, under the command of a Captain Vauclier. On entering the field to take possession of the stores, they were set upon from all sides by the hidden local men.

The seamen fought bravely, but discharged all their pieces at once and were overwhelmed before they had time to reload. They were all killed except Vauclier, their leader, who swam to the ship with a pitchfork entangled in his clothing. He was a strong man and a powerful swimmer, and he alone survived. Sir Edward was so incensed that he decided to hang the hostage, whose name was Sigerson. With constant pleading Sigerson finally convinced Sir Edward that his mother was of English descent and that the Irish would not be sorry for him if he were to be sacrificed. Eventually Sir Edward set him free. It is said that the dead Englishmen were buried on the beach. None of the attackers died in the fray. Among the locals the only one wounded was a man named O'Sullivan. At a later date Queen Elizabeth granted Sir Edward Denny six thousand acres belonging to the Earl of Desmond, and Tralee Castle.

THE RED-HAIRED FRIAR OF SCARIFF

The ancient Irish name of St Finan's Glen in the parish of Prior was Gleann Orcáin, the Glen of the Wild Boars. Here was born Francis O'Sullivan, who later became a priest of the Order of St Francis. He and his brother Dónall, a layman, fought against Cromwell in Munster. The priest succeeded in collecting money and arms, including four cannons, where others had failed to obtain help. His brother Daniel was also famous throughout Iveragh. They belonged to the 'Ceann Eiche' or 'Horse Head' Sullivans, a small clan which still survived in South Iveragh. Folklore tells that Father Francis was head of the Order of St Francis at the time he went to fight against Cromwell. He was known as An Bráthair Rua, the Red-Haired Friar of Scariff.

Scariff Island in Ballinskelligs Bay contains three hundred and sixty-five acres and once supported three families. It was good land for sheep-rearing and cattle, well sheltered on the south, and had plenty of fresh water and good fertile soil for cultivation. It had one terrible disadvantage: no beach or landing facilities, only the dangerous slanting cliff face. Only in good weather could contact be made between island and mainland.

On this island fastness Father O'Sullivan sought refuge. The country and his beloved Iveragh was overrun by the Redcoats, with Cromwell loose upon the land. The spectre of his blood-stained sword seemed to hang over the people as a fearful symbol of his authority. An edict was issued to army officers that all Roman Catholic priests living in the area or anyone who gave them shelter were to be hunted down and put to the sword. Eventually the Red-Haired Friar was captured by a party of Red-coats searching the Island. He was decapitated on the spot with a sword-swipe across the mouth, delivered by an officer of the Cromwellian garrison billeted on Valentia Island. On St John's Eve, 1658, 'his lifeblood stained the heather'. (The patriot and Gaelic poet Piaras Feiritéir was hanged at Gallows Hill, Killarney, a few years earlier.)

The upper portion of Father O'Sullivan's skull remained in the possession of the O'Connell family of Derrynane, who kept it as a treasured relic until it disappeared from the house, which now belongs to the nation. It is said that the relic returned mysteriously by parcel post bearing a British postmark some years later.

Alas! Friar of Scariff, who is left to pray for you? Who will remember the part you played? Your dirge will be the pounding surge of the grey Atlantic billows, forever thundering a protest on the rocks beneath Cuas an tSolais, the Cave of Light, and the plaintive calling of the great gull wheeling the sky above Clais na nÉamh, the Hollow of the Groans.

THE WRECK OF *THE HERCULES*

The last day and hour of December at the end of the year 1808, the sky over Ballinskelligs Bay took on a strange and frightening appearance. A great ink-black wall seemed to rise on the horizon, some parts resembling frowning fortress-like castles. There were other signs, like giant pot hooks and fingers that reached high into the heavens. The old people shook their heads and spoke in hushed voices. (This was how I heard the tale as it was handed down from knee to knee.) The wind was coming alive in the south-east, with white horses kicking their heels skyward and tossing their silver-crested manes as they careered across the bay towards the towering cliffs of Bolus. All the signs foretold a formidable hurricane. The lion was already baring its incisors, snarling and spitting pieces of iron snow into the wind, as the proud frigate *Hercules* sailed into Ballinskelligs Bay, unaware of her fate. A three-masted ship, well found and equipped with cannon on both port and starboard, *The Hercules* was a privateer licensed by the British Crown to prey on ships of the Spanish Main in the western approaches to the British Isles. Spanish ships blown off course on their way home from the West Indies were attacked and plundered by these legalized pirates, who relieved them of their rich cargoes and then destroyed them. Three sailing boats from Brittany sheltered in Ballinskelligs Bay on the same evening. These were poor French fishermen, who netted for mackerel on the south coast of Ireland. When they saw the ugly apparition enter the bay displaying the skull and cross-bones they immediately put to sea under shortened sail, rather than share harbour with the dark pirate. *The Hercules* sailed across the bay into Lúb an Rínín, the Loop of Rineen, casting two anchors near Pointe na mBiorraí, where she lay steady under the shelter of the hills for the night. But things do not always happen as man supposes; God had not yet given consent.

The night fell under the light of a full moon, which seemed to scurry across the sky, as if playing hide-and-seek between the rushing clouds. The wind now steadily increased to a full gale, and as the tide turned to flow inward from the Atlantic it attained hurricane force. From that moment on, the pirate *Hercules* was forced astern inch by inch, her anchors losing hold as she was driven across the bay. The inches became feet and the feet became fathoms. The dark pennant depicting the skull and cross-bones, the 'Jolly Roger', now began to symbolize *The Hercules*' impending doom.

After two tortured hours, she had found holding ground once more, south-east of Hector's Point, where her heavy anchors gripped again the rough rock-strewn bottom. *The Hercules* lay there until dawn broke at low water, unable to escape. The wind suddenly changed to a less favourable point, forcing her towards Cuas an Mhadra Uisce, the Water Dog's Cave. The mighty backwash from the breakers hurled itself against the low cliffs, creating a mountainous mass of disturbed water. Within this churning vortex lay the helpless ship, pounded unmercifully as each towering breaker with curling frothy lip bore down on her. Her once swashbuckling crew could be seen clinging to the rigging in terror. A raging laugh from the billows seemed to scream louder than the storm, saying, 'Ho! Ho! Mighty *Hercules*, why has your strength forsaken you?' The drama was not yet over. A large crowd on the shore watched a desperate attempt to leave the stricken vessel, as seven seamen lowered a boat that was dashed to matchwood on the cliff and its occupants drowned. Later that morning the fury of the storm abated, and *The Hercules* lay on her beam-ends, across the Water Dog's Cave.

An old pirate seized a heavy axe and chopped the main mast at deck level. Fortunately it fell onto the low cliff with its yard-arms and shrouds, creating a temporary bridge which gave the crew enough time to scramble ashore. Some time later the remains of three drowned pirates were found, and buried near the cliff face. The graves were still visible in my youth, but the sea has since claimed them back again, to rest forever within its tumultuous bosom. I do not know why they were not buried in consecrated ground. One of the pirates made a gift of his waistcoat to a local labouring man who had saved his life when he fell onto a rock as he tried to scramble ashore. It is said that the waistcoat had gold coins hidden in its fabric. The local man went missing at once, and it transpired later that he had reached America, where his progeny thrived. It surely is an ill wind that blows no good for somebody.

Some years later, the rocks at the Water Dog's Cave were exposed at low water during one of the spring tides. It happened that Mary Hoare, Francis Sigerson's maidservant, a woman both muscular and strong, usually fetched a large wooden pail of spring water from the well nearby. On this particular morning she noticed some glittering objects strewn among the rocks, and going down the rugged cliff face, she collected many pieces of gold and silver. She filled her apron and the wooden bucket, proceeded homeward and emptied her valuable cargo on to the kitchen's flagged floor. The master of the house, who was upstairs, heard the clang of metal against the floor, and came rushing down saying, 'Good girl, Mary! you have found riches. It makes a musical pure sound!' Several other pieces were found during other great tides which followed. Francis Sigerson and Maurice 'Hunting Cap' O'Connell, uncle of the Liberator, put the hoard up for public auction. The proceeds of the sale were used to buy food for the Famine survivors in the immediate area. Perhaps some of the loot still lies buried beneath the sand near the mouth of the cave, which was known from then on as Cuas an Airgid, the Cave of the Silver. Let it disintegrate beneath the mud of timelessness, because as the old saying goes, wealth is not wed to happiness, nor is all gold that glitters.

This is the story of the pirate *Hercules*, registered out of London, as I heard it by my father's fireside. I neither add nor subtract.

FAMINE AND AMERICA

I heard many gruesome Famine tales at the fireside, terrible but true, of corpses lying by the roadside in South Iveragh, their lips stained green from chewing nettle leaves and other herbs. Thousands left the countryside even up to the eighteen-fifties. Two 'side-wheelers' which had sail and steam were sent as a humane gesture by the American government of the time, to help the remaining destitute families by offering them free passage to the 'Promised Land'. Two great liners sailed up the Shannon to Limerick for this purpose only, one being the steamship SS *Jane Black*. Entire families left Ballinskelligs and the area from Cahersiveen to Bolus, Valentia Island, St Finan's Glen and Portmagee. Most of them settled on the east coast, between Boston and New Jersey. As people fled their smallholdings, the few fields where they had never experienced security of tenure, the English masters set up soup-distributing centres in some of the more stricken areas – alas! too little, too late. A large iron pot which contained one hundred gallons of beef soup, with a glowing fire beneath, was set up in the village square, and a starving populace queued up to avail of the life-giving broth. Two warm blankets, plenty of soup, and a farm cut from the best estates was offered to any Irish families who would renounce allegiance to Rome and turn to the Church of England or any of the non-Catholic persuasions.

A story is told about an old woman nicknamed 'Kate the Souper'. Kate was missing from Sunday Mass for several weeks. Rumour had it that she had forsaken her Church. One Sunday morning when the parish priest arrived to celebrate Mass, he noticed a dejected, forlorn figure sitting outside the church, with a shawl pulled over her face and head, shunned by all her friends, the pariah of the community. The priest approached her, saying, 'Welcome back, Kate! I knew you would return. Did you get the blankets, Kate?'

'I did, Father.'

'And why not, Kate! I suppose you drank as much soup as would float the *Jane Black*?'

'I did, Father, and I am sorry.'

'Come, Kate, let us offer the sacrifice of the Mass. And I will have material for a nice sermon this morning, and you will be the prodigal daughter.'

Some Irish families turned Protestant to regain lands they were deprived of by Queen Elizabeth. Others turned for the sake of wealth and rank – those who would sell their souls for a cap and a stripe. Some of the Irish 'soupers' became high-ranking officers in the king's army, and some studied medicine in Trinity College, Dublin. I remember a verse from a poem I read in my schooldays. I do not know who the author was, but it refers to the hunger of the Famine years.

> *It has gnawed like a wolf*
> *At my heart, Mother,*
> *A wolf that is fierce for blood;*
> *All the livelong day, and the night beside,*
> *Gnawing for lack of food.*
> *I dreamed of bread in my sleep, Mother,*
> *And the sight was Heaven to see;*
> *I awoke with an eager, famishing lip,*
> *But you had no bread for me.*

Emigration was the ultimate legacy of the poor. I remember the American wakes, which were sad and tearful occasions. The neighbours got together in the house of the intending emi- grant, where tea and light refreshments might be provided and the accordion played for set dancing and singing. The emigrant might be given little gifts of money to help him on his way. The friends would all stay until it was time for departing, usually for the early morning train from Cahersiveen. People who lived twelve or fifteen miles away had to travel by horse-cart or sidecar, and therefore make an early start. For a lot of them it was the last sad farewell, only some being fortunate enough to see their parents again. Many made good, but many others fell by the wayside.

*   *   *

My grand-uncles Jerry and John Kirby along with Michael Geof- frey O'Connell emigrated to the United States during the Famine year of 1847. Michael O'Connell was the husband of Ellen Kirby and a stonemason by trade. Ellen Kirby stayed at home in Ballinskelligs with her three young children. After working for three years Michael paid for their passage to join him in America. Ellen left Cobh in the year 1850 with her three children, Mary, Daniel and John, the youngest, who was only four years old. By all accounts the voyage was prolonged and stormy: in those days the normal voyage required six weeks or more. The ship was overcrowded with thousands fleeing from hunger. The O'Connell children became very seasick and one day Ellen Kirby was thrown violently to the deck suffering fracture to several of her ribs. Worst of all, little John did not survive the ordeal and when he died the great ocean received his body.

Finally the ship reached the Gulf of St Laurence where the passengers disembarked at Quebec. Michael Geoffrey O'Connell met his depleted little flock. They proceeded down the St Laurence to Montreal. A short time later they moved to Albany, staying for a while until work became scarce, whereupon they moved to Boston. Work was scarce in Boston also, and O'Connell was advised to travel south where stonemasons were in demand for building walls and milking-houses for farmers. They started to travel once more and on reaching Virginia lived some time at a place called Farmville in Prince Edward County. They moved again to Kingsport in Sullivan County, Tennessee, together with the Kirby brothers, Jerry and John. Very soon after, the American Civil War began. John Kirby enlisted with the Northern and Jerry Kirby with the Southern side, taking a horse valued at twenty-four dollars with him into the cavalry: two brothers from Ballinskelligs fighting to uphold their opposing ideals in the land of their adoption. John Kirby was killed in action at the battle of Vicksburg in May 1863. Jerry survived the war and came to live with his sister Ellen Kirby O'Connell until his death a few years later. The brothers are buried in Tennessee, as the poet has written:

> *Under the sod and the dew*
> *Awaiting the judgment day;*
> *Under the laurel the blue,*
> *Under the willow the grey.*

Many thousands fell on both sides, all honourable men in their own right, all warriors, victims of unpredictable circumstance. The story ends as Michael O'Connell and Ellen Kirby purchase a piece of land at Cropper, in Shelby County, Kentucky. They had eleven children. Ellen Kirby died in the year 1899, and her husband in 1910 at the grand old age of ninety-seven. Ellen was laid to rest in Shelbyville, and Michael in Louisville. Their many descendants still live in Kentucky, proud of their Irish ancestry, and come back occasionally to visit Ballinskelligs, whence their forebears fled. I dedicate the following verse to, Ellen Kirby's great granddaughter Nancy O'Connell Kirby and her husband Howard Maxfield.

> *This night I'm in exile*
> *Far over the foam,*
> *Away from my friends*
> *And my dear ones at home;*
> *How quickly I'd come*
> *My joy to reveal,*
> *To see once again*
> *Dear old Sceilg Mhichíl.*

THE LADY OF HORSE ISLAND

My aunt Julia Kirby lived on Horse Island. She was a tall broad-shouldered swarthy woman of the Uí Chiarmhaic clan. She well matched her name in the flesh, for Ciarmhaic means 'son of the dark one' and her eyes and hair were as black as the fruit of the sloe thorn. She married David Fitzgerald of Horse Island some time in the eighteen-sixties. Her husband died suddenly of pneumonia, leaving her with six young children, and my father went across to the island and helped her rear the young family.

Many were the tales she told of the hardship and privations suffered by the smallholders of that time. In early spring and autumn Breton fishermen arrived in sailing boats from Brest, St Malo and Concarnau to fish for the much-coveted mackerel found in abundance off the south-west coast of Ireland. They kept casks and salt on board and cured some of their catch for the Irish market. They were as destitute as were the Irish at that time, coming ashore on the island to collect bucketfuls of the striped chocolate and cream snail-shells, and filling my aunt's little kitchen where they roasted the snail-shells on the coals of the open fire. They would break the snails open, add a little salt and eat them from the palm of the hand, offering her some snails and addressing her as Mother. 'Oh Mother!' they would exclaim, 'snails plenty goot for the Mungi, they are just like butta!' They would also bring her sour black wine kept in casks, which they called 'vino claret'. The sailors virtually lived on the snails which still abound in the island's stone fences, where can be seen the brown thrushes knocking them against the rocks. Perhaps we miss out on this delicacy. The sailors all wore wooden shoes like clogs, carved from solid blocks of wood, some of them very ornate. They would row over to the mainland when the weather was suitable and pick buckets of winkles and limpets from the reefs when the tide had receded. They also fished for wrasse from the rocks and would exchange dark French tobacco with the locals for fresh milk and eggs. When the weather was not fit for fishing, they repaired their nets and sails, without which they could not operate. They often took to the fields on the shore to walk for exercise, and would sit for hours on the beach playing a card game.

One old man from Ballinskelligs called Séamus Jack would sit beside them every day while they played cards. Old Séamus seemed fascinated by hearing a foreign language, and vowed that he understood every word the sailors said, maintaining that anyone who could speak Irish well could also understand French. When asked to translate some of the games he would answer readily. One game the sailors played was just like the Irish '*Dáir an bhó*', so it meant 'Bull the cow', and the French name for the ace of hearts was '*cloch i dtóin chait*' or 'a pebble in a cat's arse'. With roguish braggadocio, he continued to show off speaking French to himself and to others in the neighbourhood.

Julia Kirby was very devout. Rain, hail or shine, she would assemble her little flock to recite the Rosary. On many evenings the sailors from Brittany joined her in prayer. When reciting the Confiteor, they answered in Latin, striking their breasts, 'Mea culpa! Mea culpa! Mea maxima culpa!' They became fast friends, the old lady of the island and the Breton fishermen.

Julia told a tale of a lone fisherman who lived on a hooker anchored in the harbour. He would arrive unexpectedly, stay for some time – perhaps days or weeks – and vanish again without trace, always putting to sea at night. He was quite deaf, but could lip-read and speak. Aunt Julia called him 'Bodharie' or 'the deaf one'. He lived entirely on fish, which he was expert in curing and drying. He would row himself to the island in a small dinghy he kept on board, and walked with a severe limp. Terra firma seemed to upset him. The children were amused with his weaving, rolling gait. Some fishermen called him 'Old Stormy': he could be seen far out to sea in very foul weather. He had a smattering of other tongues as well as Irish, but he never divulged his identity though he was constantly muttering in monotone.

One night while Bodharie's hooker lay anchored in the shelter of the island in early October, a fierce hurricane struck the coast. Later that night when the storm had abated, Julia Kirby peered out into the feeble spume-filled moonlight of the harbour but failed to see the hooker. It was gone, swept away by the power of the storm. The good lady of the island said a prayer for the old man of the sea before retiring. Later that night she was awakened by a knock on the door. She lit a candle, and asked who was outside, but received no reply. Then came a knock on the window pane, and there she beheld the half-drowned figure of old Bodharie like an apparition from the deep. She opened the door and he stumbled into the kitchen, dishevelled as a wet hen, his fingers torn and bleeding and his scanty clothing in shreds. Breaking into a mournful sobbing, he repeated over and over in Irish, '*Mo bháidín, mo bháidín,*' 'My boat, my little boat, I've lost my boat!' His hooker had been dashed to pieces but he escaped miraculously by climbing the cliff face. Julia Kirby made him comfortable while he stayed with the family, until one day he was taken on board a French boat on her way to St John's, Newfoundland, to fish for cod.

The good lady of the island lived to enjoy helping to raise her grandchildren in old age. She often went to the mainland to take up vigil beside the sick, the lonely, and the dying, bringing succour to many bent on their last journey. She suffered patiently in her own last years from an incurable infected foot. This seemed part of the pathway to sainthood: the golden domes, the jewel-studded shrines, the carved angels standing guard by the marble tombs are but dross beside a cup of water given in His Name.

Horse Island is now deserted, where generations of healthy, happy families were once reared. Present-day economics make island life impossible.

THE GREAT SNOWSTORM

One fine evening in February 1898, a light wind came from the fern-clad hills of the east, blowing directly across the sea and into the little fishing village of Ballinskelligs. The weather was neither cold nor wintry, although flakes of dry snow were scattered on the wind. I heard my uncle John Cremin say that windows of blue appeared in the north-eastern sky as night was falling, while spittles of hard powder-like snow wafted wraith-like from out of the east. Not even the most seasoned weather forecasters – the village wise men, the 'know-alls', 'I told you so's,' 'I could see that coming for days,' 'the cat had his rump to the fire all last week' – not one foretold the blizzard of the century. So the people of Ballinskelligs retired for the night without fear of any great change in the weather.

Many grew impatient in their beds, complaining that the dawn had not shown in the windows, nor was the cock crowing as usual. Each house seemed shrouded in everlasting night. When my father's patience came to an end he unbolted the cottage door. He got the shock of his life when a great wall of powdery snow forced him backwards and tumbled across the floor. It half filled the kitchen up to the open hearth. Six or seven feet of snow had fallen during the night, shutting off all daylight.

My father was lucky to have the big shovel in the kitchen that night. He immediately started to dig his way into the open until he exposed the windows to let the light filter through. He worked all morning and most of the day, shovelling snow, digging a pathway to the haggard and the cowhouse and finally to the spring well, which was some distance from our house. You could see only the outline of the thatched cottages, and the blue smoke of the turf fire rising from each chimney. A neighbour who once lived in Canada compared it to a scene from the Yukon. The whole countryside was transformed overnight into a land of dazzling whiteness, with not an inch of green remaining.

It had been a market and fair day in Cahersiveen, ten miles away. Most people who went to the cattle sale were caught in the blizzard on their way home. The snow had risen above the level of the fields, and there was no trace of the road to be seen. People had to abandon their carts, leading the horses who floundered in the deep snow, and carrying what commodities they had purchased on their backs. One group had arrived within a mile of home, when the powdery, suffocating snow was falling so heavily that they were forced to abandon their wagons. My neighbour Michael Sugrue told of his father John's return that evening. There happened to be one mule among the troupe, which proved superior to the horse in its sense of direction, never straying off the centre of the roadway. The men decided to take all weight off the creature's body, and drive it ahead on a lead rope. The mule moved in slow plunging strides, step by step, yard by yard, until finally it reached the safety of a roadside cottage.

I heard my father say that bird life suffered. He would go out and dig in the black soil, and immediately flocks of different birds would surround him while he dug. Song-birds of every description were in quest of seed, worms or grubs. My father was expert at constructing clever bird-traps from pieces of old fishing nets. Snipe were numerous, and golden and grey plover were also good to eat. Every other day they had a pot of snipe or plover for dinner. The weather continued very severe for most of the winter and spring, so cold that many wild fowl died of starvation. Every night starlings would nestle on the thatched roof near the chimney to catch the warmth of the smoke rising from the turf fire.

Many were the tales told of sheep that survived burial beneath snowdrifts for long periods. Snow remained on the Reeks of Kerry, Ireland's highest mountains, until July, and was piled high on the Crag of the Dog on Canuig Mountain until June of that year. A hot summer compensated for the snowfall of the century.

IN QUEST OF HAPPINESS:
A TRAVELLER'S TALE

I once knew a man whom we called 'Paddy the Hill', a man who had travelled to foreign parts and spent many years in quest of wealth. After failing to find riches he at last found happiness in being poor. He lived in a small house, in an out-of-the-way place at the far end of the glen. The cottage looked as if it wanted to cuddle itself in under the craggy shelf of Canuig Mountain. Its two windows peered out from the shadows of seclusion.

On one of the many lingering rainy days suitable only for staying indoors, I paid a visit to Paddy the Hill. Getting up from his chair by the open fire, he made me welcome, saying, 'Sit up near the heat, and tell me the latest story.'

'It is the old custom', said I, 'that the man of the house must tell the first story.'

Paddy burst into laughter. 'Ho! Ho!' he exclaimed, 'How clever of you! Aristotle! Yes! it was Aristotle who said that! You're perfectly right: I'm trapped already. I had the qualifications of a schoolteacher when I left home. I was twenty-two years old and anxious to travel. I walked all the way to Dublin, where I expected to find work, but I spent days on end searching the city to no avail. Only when my money was running out did I find a job as a "coal trimmer" on board a trading vessel bound for Liverpool. It was better than nothing but it was a most unhealthy job, breaking down large lumps of coal and making it ready for the stokers who fed the furnaces. It did not require much education to trim coal. Very soon I became as black as the coal itself, and I was drowned in my own perspiration and smeared with sour vomit. To make matters worse, the stokers hurled a perpetual tirade of obscenities at me. The voyage to Liverpool was dogged by storms. We hove to for twenty-four hours outside Dublin until the weather improved, after which we developed trouble from a leaking boiler before finally limping into Liverpool. The captain paid me fifteen shillings for the voyage.

'I left the dock and walked down the street. Weakened by seasickness, I did not present a pretty sight to the first person I met. This happened to be a well-dressed young woman who inquired if I had come off the ship which had just docked, and if I intended staying at the Seaman's Institute. I told her it was my first time outside of Ireland, and that I was grateful for her concern on my behalf. She assured me that it was part of her job: she worked for the society. She accompanied me to the Seaman's Institute where I had a bath and changed into clean clothes. She also told me her parents were Irish, but that she was born in Liverpool. She was a cheerful person with a wonderful singing voice, and she constantly hummed the haunting air of "Where the River Shannon Flows". Next morning as I walked along the street I saw a notice which read "Jobs Vacant" in large letters, displayed outside a tavern called "The Crow's Nest". I went inside, bought a drink, and asked the barman if I could have a look at the "Jobs Vacant" list. One notice read: "Young man or boy, wanted immediately as cook's helper with general galley chores;

apply at dock shipping office, SS *Star of India*, sailing to Singapore."

'Before long I found myself speaking with the boatswain of the *Star of India*. He turned me over to the head steward, who fine-combed me with questions and said that as far as he was concerned I was suitable for the job. After the ship's doctor had vaccinated me and given me a medical once-over, I signed the ship's roster accepting the conditions of contract. The girl from the Institute came with me to the dockside that evening, whispering, "Please don't leave. I'll get you a shore job here in Liverpool." I assured her I would come back, and she bade me goodbye at the foot of the great ship's gangway, holding my hand, and singing the last lovely lines of "Where the River Shannon Flows" with tears in her eyes. Many a day afterwards was I haunted by those clear flowing notes, like the brown thrush of Ireland.

'It was little I thought that evening as I sailed out of Liverpool that the hand of fate had already decided my lot in life, and that many suns would rise and set before I would realize my ambition of richness or happiness. Five long weeks elapsed before I set foot on land again. I worked in the galley helping the cook. During the first week I was so constantly seasick that I sometimes wished the ship would founder and thereby end my misery. The smell of cooking and even the sight of food triggered off prolonged bouts of vomiting. After eight days in this condition I was in an emaciated state, and one day I collapsed in the galley. An old sailor suggested that I must vomit until I got rid of all the poisonous bile: when this is gone you are free from the seasickness forever. He gave me a potion with such a rotten taste that I will never forget it. After taking the first sip, my stomach reacted so violently I thought I would actually turn inside out, but the spasms squeezed the last drop of green acid from my gut. The old sailor stayed with me, giving me little sips of boiled water with a tiny pinch of salt. I fell into a peaceful sleep and when I awakened I felt much refreshed. The lines in "The Ancient Mariner" seemed like sleep made into music:

Oh sleep! it is a gentle thing,
Beloved from pole to pole!
To Mary Queen the praise be given!
She sent the gentle sleep from Heaven,
That slid into my soul.

'From that day on I never again experienced seasickness. I asked the old sailor what was in his secret potion. "Paddy," he replied, "if you must know, only a small drop of vinegar mixed with one rotten egg." I nearly got the spasms again.

'The crew who worked the ship were mostly Lascars, but the master and his officers were British. The cook was a middle-aged Welshman from Cardiff. He was the captain's favourite, and he was very good to me. The chief engineer was the only other Irishman on board. The officers played cards and drank in the captain's saloon, often until late at night, except when they were on watch. I was detailed to bring them snacks on these occasions. These men were forever discussing sex and prostitutes. It was strange to listen to men who were like beings apart from the female world. These "deepwater men" are never happy living on shore. Some look on women with awe, while others are obsessed by sexual desire. Many a strange tale was swapped, exciting, incredible tales of distant ports they had visited: the bazaars of India, the harems of the Orient and the opium dens of Hong Kong.

'It was perhaps unwise of me to come ashore in India. As the old saying goes "Lonely is he in a foreign land without food or a friend near his shoulder, for the day of the feud, the blame will lie heavy on him." In any case, I bade farewell to my new-found friends and to the sea in the teeming city of Bombay. I was lonely leaving the big ship which had brought me safely across the ocean. I looked back at her tall masts, her great red, white and blue funnels, her majestic white bridge and superstructure, and I was seized by a sudden nostalgic whim. For a brass pin, I would have gone back to my job in the galley. More's the pity I didn't, for I felt suddenly alone once more. The soles of my feet still burned with the itch of wanderlust, but I was yet to learn of the dangerous pitfalls that lay in store. When I left the ship, I possessed twenty-five pounds, some of which I had won in card games: the crew played a simple game called "sweep", not unlike poker. Twenty-five pounds was a fortune in India. You could buy a camel and a woman for three pounds in those days.

'Bombay was teeming with people: street-traders, beggars clutching at your arm, whining and asking for alms. In the bazaars and in the open market, fruit and vegetables were readily available. There was brassware of every description, oriental rugs, carpets and silks, exotic birds in gilded cages, cheap and expensive jewellery, fakirs, trick-of-the-loop-men and snake-charmers. A turbaned Indian squatted on a rug, playing on a long ebony lute; a deadly cobra coiled up on the rug in front of the musician, weaving its head to and fro, hypnotized by its master. The sight of this sent chills up my spine. The mystery and mysticism of the East surpasses normal understanding. It is like a glimpse into the past. Pickpockets were numerous, their hands as delicate as silk. A soothsayer painted an accurate picture of my future, which I dismissed as nonsense. He warned me not to go into the interior, especially to the north to a city whose name started with D. He also told me that he heard people calling to me: "Do not go into the bazaar to buy something; if you do you will not be lucky." I should have taken heed of what he said, for there is an old saying that the best advice is given and never asked for.

'I learnt a smattering of the language. I had not spent much of my money so far; I purchased only a canvas tent with bamboo poles. I dressed myself in Hindu clothing, letting my hair grow and my beard become a long pointed black tress hanging from my chin. My face was thin and long-featured, and my skin, burnt red from the sun, was like shrivelled leather. With a white turban on my head, a white cotton sarong, and a loose pair of white pants, on my oath! my own mother would not have recognized me! I found employment in the big cotton mill near the harbour. It was the store where raw cotton was compressed and bound into packs of one hundredweight. It was my job to count and label the finished rolls, which were ready for export. Very soon I was recognized as well-educated and good at figures. The Indian workers called me "Sahib". I worked there for three years. One day, I decided to write to my mother and send her a gift. I went to the bazaar, where beautiful wraps were on display, to buy a silken shawl. Just as I was about to buy the shawl I had chosen, misfortune struck. An Indian dressed in spotless cotton suddenly confronted me, while two others stood by my side like soldiers. I tried to leave, but one man placed a hand on my arm saying, "Do not be afraid! We do not intend to harm you. Please do our bidding." I was escorted up a narrow laneway which led into a wide yard like an old market-place.

'I was surprised to see three magnificent full-grown elephants standing in line, with a keeper in charge. Each majestic creature had rich trappings, with colourful rugs on their broad backs and shoulders. The cradle was made of polished ebony, inlaid with ivory and covered by a canopy of white silk, while pendants of silver and gold hung from the edges. The elephants knelt on the ground at the command of the keeper: what gentle passive animals they seemed to be! I took my seat on the silken cushions of the howdah. Before starting to leave, the spokesman explained the mystery of my captivity. "We are ordered by His Majesty the Rajah to take you to his palace. He wishes to speak to you, because he requires a schoolteacher from the West to instruct his sons in European culture. He had information about your qualifications. Do not regard this as a hostile act, for you will be well paid and well cared for."

'This explanation eased my fears, but I was still worried about what lay in store. We started on our journey into the country. We travelled through very flat plains where many acres were under rice and cotton. There were no small green fields such as we see in Ireland. To the north the snow-capped peaks of mountains were visible, although miles and miles distant. It seemed so strange in the summer heat to see towering, glistening spires of white, shining among the clouds on the distant horizon. This was a vast country with gigantic mountains. The midday heat was oppressive although we were protected by the canopy of the howdah. The elephants now walked at a slow pace and the road became narrow and winding. We travelled through small groves of stunted scrub and little hillocks, where I saw multicoloured butterflies, and black lizards basking in the intense heat and slithering across the pathway to avoid being trodden on by the elephants. The path led us through a country village not unlike an Irish one. Tall handsome women carried waterjars on their heads, walking gracefully upright. Peasants worked in the fields, some ploughing the brown soil with primitive ox-drawn wooden ploughs. The earth seemed brittle and loose. Others made red bricks from clay. It became more evident that we were approaching the end of our journey. Very soon we passed near a garden which had fountains of crystal water bursting heavenward. The lawns were full of coloured blossom and tropical palms: I had never seen such beauty. The elephants walked in line between high ornamental gates of shining brass and ivory. Then the palace of the Rajah came into view, a picture in gleaming columns of dazzling white marble, which had veins of blue and dark red traced like branches of exotic fruit-trees. The afternoon sun reflected shafts of brilliant light off the highly polished mirror that was the Rajah's palace.

'There, servants told me to bathe and to put on the garb which had been provided. Two young girl servants beckoned me to follow them into a luxurious washroom, fragrant with roses and incense. The girls asked me to remove all my clothing, which they said must be incinerated to comply with palace hygiene. I became fearful and shy because I had never exposed my body in the presence of females. I stripped to the waist, telling the girls they must leave the room, and that I intended to wash on my own. One girl replied, "You must obey palace rules, please! Do not make life difficult for yourself." However, I persisted in my stubborn attitude, so she said, "Be prepared for a shock – you have only yourself to blame." Thereupon she struck several notes with a bamboo rod on a brass bell. A side door opened and I beheld a muscular giant, his beard hanging from his chin like the tail of an ass. After some brief words with the girls he grasped both my arms, exerting a vice-like pressure which rendered me immobile. He relieved me of my trousers in one fell swoop. He then laid me gently into a scented bath, as naked as the day I was born, delivering a slap on the bottom such as is given to a child, and saying, "Now, behave yourself!" The girls washed every inch of my body, and manicured my toenails and fingernails. I was then massaged with a fragrant cooling ointment. A hairdresser cut my beard in classical Indian style, giving me an air of importance; he took away all beard from the centre of my chin, leaving Chinese pigtails hanging at the sides. This was the eastern hairstyle which denoted the wise man or scribe. Then entered two doctors who listened to my breathing and took some blood from one of my fingertips. One doctor examined my testicles, giving the strings a sudden downward pull which caused me backache. They then informed me that they would perform a slight operation, so that I could not become fruitful with any of the special female caste in the palace. I was given a drink to prepare me for the sterilization I was to undergo on the morrow. My spirits plunged to the depths of despair on hearing of the disfigurement proposed for my manhood. I would rather be dead. When the ablutions were finished, I was dressed in a sarong of white cotton and a coloured turban, with soft leopardskin slippers on my feet. I was taken before the Rajah. He was seated on a chair fashioned from ivory tusks, throne-like in design. I bowed low to his greeting, and he ordered the manservant to bring me food.

'I was given several different kinds of tasty meat and fish with breads and fruit. I relished the fine meal, for I was ravenous after a long fast, in spite of fear and uncertainty. The Rajah explained that he intended setting up a school in the palace, to prepare his children, especially his two sons, for western European culture. He told me there was only a small stumbling-block to my appointment: it would be necessary to sterilize me, to prevent any pollution of the caste system within the palace. I felt a cold shiver creep up my spine. The left testicle would be removed, he said, and assured me that I would be well paid and would not suffer any pain.

'"I will reward you with riches you have never dreamed of," he added. He then ordered his servants to give me special attention at all times. Next I was shown my sleeping quarters. Fortunately for me my bedroom was at the rear of the palace overlooking the servants' quarters, which had a separate back garden and entrance.

My bed was a low four-poster with a silken tasselled canopy. The room was very comfortable, with many cushions and wall hangings. I noticed it was on the second floor, about fifteen feet above ground level. I was planning my escape already, having resolved that I would leave immediately. I would rather die now than let them desecrate my body. I always heard that God's help is nearer than the door: an old Irish saying said so. One of the girls who had washed me entered the room as light-footed and as ghostly as a moonbeam: she startled me. In her hand she held a small bag. "Would you wish to escape?" she asked in a whisper. "This is for you, hurry take it! Come at once! You must go back to Bombay! The night is short: if you are missed, the hounds will pursue you. I will escort you into the open and by the sentry in the garden: he will not challenge us, for he is my secret lover."

'She grasped my hand and was leading me down a back staircase, when we heard the Rajah on his way up, accompanied by one of the palace guards. I felt my heart jump into my mouth, but as quick as light the girl pulled me around a corner and into a little alcove.

'"Keep low and don't breathe," she whispered. They swept by us. I thought my lungs would burst; my heart drummed, tum, tum, tum. God be praised! the road seemed to open once more, and we almost ran down the rest of the stairway, which led into the shrubbery, and up a short marble staircase. A dog recognized the girl and wanted to fawn on her and lick her hand. We walked away into the open, past the guard who strolled in the opposite direction to us.

'The night had just fallen when she bade me stop. She put her warm arms around my neck and kissed me. Her kiss seemed like the seal of my freedom. She whispered, "Kneel and say three times, 'Praise be to Allah of grace!'" Then, kneeling beside me, she said: "Do you see that big star in the south? Keep that star on your left, until you see the lights of Bombay reflected in the sky." She handed me another little bag and vanished as if the ground had swallowed her.

'I was alone. About twenty-five miles separated me from the city in which I had made some new friends. The night was sultry, and a little crescent moon hung low in the western sky. From now on I must navigate for myself. Searching the little sack, I found to my surprise a very sharp dagger and a pair of leather slippers. I changed into these, and they offered more protection from thorns than the cloth slippers of the palace. I made steady progress, walking as fast as possible through a rough growth of sedge-like reed. It is an old saying that a good running horse must stumble some time. Suddenly I saw two blue-green lights directly in my path, and I heard the snarling hiss of the cheetah. I lurched quickly to the right. Fortunately it leaped clear of my shoulder, disappearing into the night. I shivered with fear of the wild, conscious of the danger of stepping on a snake or some other dangerous creature. By this time two hours must have passed, and I had covered perhaps ten miles. I calculated that dawn should show in the eastern sky in another hour and a half. The young moon had dipped below the distant horizon long before. The faint rosy glow I noticed through the night haze of the southern sky raised my spirits: perhaps it was the reflection of the city lights which the Indian girl had spoken of. Praise be to Allah of grace, perhaps I would come safe after all.

The dawn broke suddenly, like thunder on my heels, seeming to follow from the east. Noticing the edge of some dense scrub, a distance to my right, I accelerated to a sprint and never stopped until I lost the light of day, deep in a jungle of thorn bushes and small trees. Fearful that a search party would recapture me, I made sure that I was hidden from daylight. It took some time for my eyes to become accustomed to my surroundings, to the strange dark green light and the smell of the jungle. I could discern branches over my head, and I used the dagger to scrape away the dangerous thorns. I laid some broken branches crosswise and pulled myself up to a crudely fashioned platform, where I placed the little sacks under my head, and though my bed was full of hard lumps, it was good to be alive and in one piece, and still hopeful. I fell into an exhausted sleep.

'In my sleep I had a vivid dream of being back in Ireland in my mother's house. She embraced me, saying, "Come home, and do not hanker after riches: this world is full of woe, and the happiness of riches is only fleeting." I could see her kneeling in prayer, a lighted candle near her, clothed in her blue apron and black woollen wrap, just as on the day I left home. She stretched out her hands to me, saying, "Come home where happiness awaits you." I awoke, cold sweat poured from my face and brow. I know now that it was at this very same time that my mother died.

'I had no idea of how long I had slept, but I identified the trumpeting of elephants on the left of the thicket. I swung down from my perch as lightly as possible, and crept forward to the edge of the jungle, just in time to see three elephants passing to the south-east. A hundred thanks to God, they were on the wrong trail. I felt as refreshed as the mythical warrior who had slept for seven days and seven nights. The sun had climbed beyond the zenith, and would soon be showing the other side of the world that a new day was dawning. Only ten miles separated me from Bombay. I was eager for night to come once more. I climbed back into the branches to get the straw bag given to me in the palace. The bag contained some sandwiches, some fish and meat, and a bottle of water. I prayed to God to bestow every favour on the girl who had befriended me.

As I let myself down from the tree platform, I felt something soft underfoot, and in an instant I felt a most terrible constricting sensation in my midriff. I was being squeezed to death by the largest snake in India, the python. My breath came in short gasps as I heard the hissing of this terrible monster, like a demon cry from Hell. My right arm was free, but the dagger was in my belt. With a supreme effort I tore it free, and plunged it sideways into the belly-like curve of one of the many coils he had wound around my middle. I managed to get the flat blade between my navel and the backbone of the serpent; this was a dangerous operation, for I had to avoid giving myself a wound, and the blade was razor-sharp on both sides. I cut the loop in two. I could breathe more freely now, but the battle was not over yet. His great head was weaving under my left armpit. I plunged the dagger into his nearest eye and upwards into his brain, where I kept twisting the weapon until I heard the grating of steel against bone. Little by little I felt the snake relax its constricting muscles. A great balloon of intestines, like inflated bicycle-tubes, burst from the wound: the guts and slimy matter covered my entire face.

'I can't describe the horrible wild smell. The hissing had ceased though there was still an occasional convulsion. I cut away the last winding coil of its narrow tail from my thigh, and stepped free from the gory mess. I stumbled into the blinding sunlight where I retched in disgust. I cleaned away as much as possible of the slimy paste which stained my clothing. Then I went back to the scene of my encounter to retrieve my bag. Sitting in the sunlight I finished the last sandwich and drank the remainder of the water, before hiding the empty bottle. My stomach and rib-cage felt sore for several days.

'The sun was now low in the clouds of the western sky. I was still trembling as I started south once more. I prayed to Jesus and His Holy Mother; I prayed also for the Hindu girl, who undoubtedly saved my life by giving me the dagger. The lights of Bombay appeared nearer by the mile. In another half-hour I should be nearing the suburbs of the city. I was so tired I scarcely noticed people on the streets as I entered the section where I lived, or that the dogs slunk away because of the odour of reptile which I exuded. After arriving at my lodgings I climbed the stairs to my room where I cast off my polluted palace clothing, and washed myself thoroughly. The weariness of my ordeal fell heavily on my eyelids. As I laid myself to rest, I imagined I heard the distant music of angels, reminding me of Shakespeare's words, "And flights of angels sing thee to thy rest."

'I resumed work in the cotton mill for some weeks more before joining the British Army in Delhi, where I spent five years in an Irish regiment, the Munster Fusiliers. My army career is another story entirely. I came back to Liverpool in a troop-ship with my regiment. We were disbanded, and badly rewarded for our services.

'Strange are the events of this life. As I stepped from the gangway in Liverpool, I heard the voice of a woman singing for pence as she moved among soldiers, sailors and drunks. Where had I heard that plaintive voice before, singing "Where the River Shannon Flows"? Memories came flooding back: the *Star of India* and the girl from the Seaman's Institute! Her face was old and worn. I had a good sum of money in my pocket, and I pressed it all into her hand. She looked at me vacantly, said, "God bless you, that you may find the happiness you are seeking," and disappeared into the crowd. I arrived back in Ireland without the riches I had sought, but here in my cottage near the mountain I find happiness again.'

Paddy the Hill glanced through the window. The rain had ceased. 'I would not exchange my cottage for the Rajah's palace,' said he, 'because this world is full of woe, and happiness stays not long.'

V
Customs and Beliefs

A FAMILY WAKE

The old man tormented and grey will die,
And die will the beautiful lark of the hill,
The youth will go and his wisdom leave behind,
And all who live shall vanish into everlasting time.

I first became acquainted with death on the evening that my grandmother Mary Fitzgerald Cremin died. Her house was near ours, only two acres or so to the west. I was with my mother at her bedside. The date was 17 September 1915. She was eighty-nine years old, and even if the signs of feeble age said that death had conquered, the lines of a once gentle maiden were still in evidence. The priest had left, having anointed her and administered the last rites. Her face had assumed a dark greyish colour. A parchment mask seemed to cover her features and the grin of the unmerciful reaper was plain to be seen on her cheeks. Several neighbouring women attended at her deathbed. They said the Rosary aloud while one of them held a lighted blessed candle in her hand. The flickering of the candle-flame was the only light in the bedroom, and ghostly shadows danced across the lime-washed walls. In the centre of the bed I could see my grandmother's face. It had now changed completely: the dark mask of death had vanished and she looked radiant with peace and grace, her fine features of polished marble like a sleeping queen's, her breath coming in a series of short sighs, with no death-rattle, no prolonged agony. My grandmother died like a baby going to sleep.

My uncles Aindí Fada and Tadhg Phats were busy hanging white sheets on the side walls near the back door. They then placed two tables end to end and covered them with more sheets and a plentiful supply of pillows, some edged with beautiful home-made lace. When all was in order, my grandmother's bier was like a scene from the time of the Pharaohs. My aunt Nell, who had just arrived home from America, told us that the undertakers over there were using paint and powder for many a day.

Some time later I noticed the women going into a huddle and whispering. They were preparing for keening the loved one who had just died. They then approached the corpse and in unison started the mournful lamentation or *caoineadh*. The cry would reach a climax, hover for a brief moment at the highest note, then descend to the depths of desolate heart-rending lamentation, each sob getting weaker and shorter until it became a stuttering moan. Being only nine years old and having never experienced keening of the dead, I became so frightened that I went through the kitchen door like a bolt of lightning, and God never stayed me until I was safe and sound again on my father's hearth. He was in the kitchen, saw my distress and sat near me to explain gently that keening the dead was a very old custom, and maybe if the truth were known most of these women were not sad at all nor shedding real tears, but putting on a show to perpetuate an old custom. At first I thought it an odd explanation, but it did not take me many years to understand that my father was right.

My mother came looking for me and took me back to the wake. Uncle Aindí and Tadhg Phats had arrived back with a large cask of porter, a box of white clay pipes and several blocks of plug tobacco. In another box I saw some bottles of red whiskey and loaves of baker's bread and crocks of red jam. The women and the men were given tea and baker's loaf with plenty of fresh butter and jam. Some men arranged seating with stools and wide thick planks of wood. The neighbours filled the last inch of space inside the kitchen. Two boys were kept busy shredding tobacco and filling clay pipes which were presented one to each person. Very soon clouds of tobacco smoke filled the room.

Some time later Aindí and Tadhg Phats came in carrying two large buckets of porter with white caps of creamy foam. Every man was given a pint glass of it. It was good to watch them swallowing great draughts, which sometimes left a beard of foam on their chins. I got a terrible longing to taste a drop of it myself, as the sweet scent of apples seemed to fill the kitchen. Not one word of English was spoken at grandmother's wake that night. The girls and the older women wore long skirts, black woollen stockings to the knee, and black shawls, with the odd brown or yellow shawl among them.

I remember listening to Aindí Fada and Tadhg Phats discussing local affairs. They both liked their drop, and usually waxed eloquent and philosophical – I suspect they were helping themselves generously from the buckets. Merry or not, they were the essence of conviviality. When all the old topics were exhausted – gardening, fishing, women, even horse-racing and regattas – and I thought that the last word was said, my uncle Aindí uttered a yawning moan, so deep and sad that one would think it came from the nethermost end of his gut. '*Ochón*,' he sighed. 'I wonder who will be here to wake us when we die?'

'Maybe, Aindí', said Tadhg Phats, 'you won't need any wake or funeral.'

'How could that happen?' asked Aindí.

'Well,' said Tadhg Phats, 'supposing you were lost at sea and your body wasn't found: maybe only the porpoise and the spike dogfish would be at your wake.'

'Now Tadhg,' exclaimed Aindí, 'don't talk like that. If you were a proper Christian you would never drown, and you would never fear the sea pigs, the dolphins or the dogfish.'

'What connection has Christianity with the subject?' asked Tadhg Phats.

'Hold on now,' said Aindí. 'It's like this. Peter the Apostle was able to walk on the water while he had confidence in Christ.'

Tadhg Phats answered with a great burst of laughter. 'On my soul, Aindí, whatever St Peter may have done, it will be a long time before we see you walking ashore from the Skelligs.'

The neighbours were enjoying this talk and they all laughed. At that moment my mother announced she was going to say the Rosary of the Virgin Mary. It was now midnight and she led the neighbours through each decade and then the Litany, imploring the saints in Heaven to intercede for the departed souls. The night was now getting late and I was feeling tired, so my mother took me home, but grandmother's death stayed planted in my memory until this present day. May you have a bed in Paradise, grandmother.

OLD MEDICINES

My father was well known for his ability to apply mustard-plasters to relieve congestion of the lungs, now called pneumonia. He was often called on by neighbours to help those suffering from difficulty in breathing, or high temperature. His treatment was a severe one which raised large water-blisters on the area affected. People knew nothing about a virus for many years to come. Doctors were few and lived only in towns. Roads and transport were very poor. Sometimes the mustard-plasters worked with a few other 'do-it-yourself' remedies thrown in. One had to be tough to risk getting sick in those days.

The old people had many traditional remedies, and superstition was mixed with home-made cures. Some went back to pre-Christian days: spells, charms, incantations, and long tracts written in the form of pagan prayer, in the blood of an ox or of the invalid. At the very least, people believed you should not make a spell or break a spell. My father often told us not to believe in spirits or ghosts or in the nether world, telling us not to be afraid of darkness just because we couldn't see plainly.

I remember having as my companion a shaggy dog called Dando. He was a loving creature. We went everywhere together. If I sat on a fence or by the river bank he never let slip the opportunity of placing his front paws on my shoulder and licking my ear. An old woman of the roads to whom we were charitable would visit us from time to time. 'Nell of the Roads' was sturdy and squat with a raucous voice. An inveterate pipe-smoker, she also liked a drop of spirits and would sometimes arrive at the house late at night. Dando must have known the old lady for several years and had never appeared aggressive towards her, but on this occasion, he committed the black crime of tasting the flesh of poor Nell's collop, which refused to heal in spite of salves, unctions and ointments. Nell herself suggested that the only cure left was to apply a piece of hair and skin from Dando's rump to the wound. Who has not heard the old saying, 'Take a hair of the dog that bit you'? My father did not believe in such nonsense and refused point-blank to become involved in the dark ritual, but with Nell's persistent pleading he finally succumbed. He tied up Dando, muzzled and trussed him like a Christmas turkey, cauterized an old razor with a flaming piece of wood, and in a jiffy removed a piece of bloody skin and hair about the size of a postage stamp from Dando's sitting part. I remember feeling sorry for my companion, a grudging donor for the last Stone Age transplant in Ballinskelligs. In the end he only squealed a little and licked his bottom very carefully when released. Nell applied the cure of ages. Wonder of wonders! her collop started to heal and soon new soft tissue covered the wounded area. Dando and Nell remained fast friends. A little square showed on the dog's rear part on which the hair never grew. As to the black magic which my father was forced to partake in, he often laughed and shook his head about it.

Another cure for boils, pimples and carbuncles was fresh goosedroppings or better still gander-droppings. They were collected while fresh from geese grazing on a green field, left in a jar until they developed a grey fuzzy growth, and then mixed with some unsalted butter. The ointment prepared in this way was especially good for drawing the centre from the carbuncle or abscess.

The gander had a very special power in the case of thrush, a disease of the throat: the beak of the gander would be inserted in the invalid's throat until the gander had breathed. Another cure for thrush was milk from which a ferret or polecat had drunk. The breath or saliva of a man who had never seen his father, or of a seventh son, had the same healing power. The tongue of a fox (cured in salt) was applied to infected wounds to draw out the pus and reduce inflammation. Very few villages would be without salted fox tongue, and neighbours shared the remedy with each other. Melted seal blubber was applied as a cure for sprains and fractures.

Country people were well versed in the use of herbal medicine. Many different species of plants were used. Few today praise the healing properties of comfrey, spear tongue, king fern root, penny leaves, yarrow, red dandelion and other plants too numerous to mention. We have only a scanty knowledge of the vast potential for man's benefit in nature.

What a great difference has taken place in dentistry since the day of 'Tim of the Sparks' who served as public dentist for the country people. At that time, chewing on a live frog's leg until you tasted its bone marrow was the cure for toothache. Conjunctivitis, red weeping eyes and granulated lids were cured by the simple application of wild honey. If a person suffered from tender or inflamed feet, he would boil bladder wrack in sea water and bathe them in it: that would soon harden his feet for the road.

A superstition handed down from pre-Christian days as an infallible cure for whooping cough was this. If you had this malady you were to look out for a rider on a grey horse and on meeting the equestrian you were to address him thus:

> *Thou rider of the grey steed*
> *What may cure my whooping cough?*

Whatever remedy he might prescribe on the spur of the moment would be an unfailing cure. It happened that a local housewife was severely stricken with the horrid cough and confined to bed with continuous spasms of the dry wheezing, which always ended with a long whooping intake of air, like the wail of a siren. She implored her husband to go into the street and keep watch for a rider on a grey steed. Her husband obeyed and waited patiently for several hours. At last he saw a rider on a grey steed approaching, but his joy was short-lived because he remembered that his wife and the rider had not been on very sweet terms for many a long day. But 'I'll chance it anyway,' said he, 'for better or worse.' He asked his question, whereupon the rider replied:

> *Butter and wine*
> *And on the bed*
> *Lay your wife, nine times.*

The tale went on to relate how quickly the woman recovered.

MATCHMAKING

An old saying has it that marriage is as much of a gamble as buying a lottery ticket. An arranged marriage, or *cleamhnas,* was a contract between a man and a woman arranged by a go-between called a *stóicín* or matchmaker. Many an old bachelor got a good wife in this manner. A man might be middle-aged before his father and mother parted with the holding. The heir, usually the eldest son, had to wait, maybe until there was snow on the roof, and not much fire in the furnace. Once the farm was signed over to him, he at last found that he was free to marry. Oh, what a relief! He was walking on air already, his step became light as a feather. He was not thinking of an old hatchet-faced prima donna who had laid her last egg. Oh no! He was dreaming of a young maiden, a beautiful, stately, silent, bashful creature. Next market day he would show them, he'd wear a white shirt and bow-tie, a new tweed suit and overcoat and new boots of boxcalf leather that the neighbours could hear the creaking of as he swung jauntily down the street. Don't mention expense! He had money galore in the bank, with acres broad and free.

Only one thing was wanting, the most important requisite of all, a partner in life, a wife. Ah yes! The years were slipping by, like grains of sand from an hourglass. Already flakes of snow were on the roof. He must hurry. He must have a talk with the matchmaker. There were a lot of important issues. He would like a girl with some money, the more the merrier: it would make the bargain much more flexible. There would be no problem about land: his farm was the best in the parish. Other important questions must be answered. 'Did the mare ever lose a shoe?' If she did, all the better for future generations. Was the potential groom in good health? Had he the fee for the matchmaker? The fee for the priest? A private room for Mom and Dad with a supply of milk and vegetables from the farm while they lived? Compensation in money to his younger brother and sister? Every point must be legally adhered to in the marriage contract. Every little detail must be correct, but not one word was yet mentioned about love.

This was a cold contract, the matchmaker's job. The bride-to-be and the bridegroom had little contact with each other until they met for better or for worse in the marriage bed that night. Now they must try and be happy with their lot, whether the tide of love filled to high-water mark or not. A sad mistake to try and weld a cold contract into a miracle of passionate love.

The matchmaker needed to be very crafty and well versed in the finer points of his trade to coax two strangers to join in matrimony. On the other hand it would be quite easy to draw up a contract between families who knew each other's background, and where the girl and boy were young and good-looking: they were usually on fire with the prospect of walking up the aisle. The matchmaker made some very easy contracts, too, for example between an elderly pair said to have long since gone beyond the limit as regards an heir to the throne. But the gossips might be in for a shock, and the local doctor himself, called to attend at the birth of bouncing twins. The village pump would be agog with the astonishing news, but the mouths of the belittlers and the wise ones were shut for ever.

The man who was called the matchmaker said nothing. He knew his job: some were happy, some were sorry 'until death do us part'. The era has flown. No longer will the farmer be seen some weeks before Easter taking his daughter to the market in the pony and trap, with the wise ones remarking, 'He has a heifer for show!'

They did not then have marriage counselling by professor or cleric, or advice on how to bring up children. Sex was not talked about, just left to human instinct. Today the whole scene has changed. Ignorance can no longer be used as an excuse for broken marriages and sexual behaviour. Couples get advice on family planning and on how to use their dangerous sexual organs. What a great social change in a century.

Eoghan Rua Ó Súilleabháin was once asked, as a great poet and a man who knew women, what kind of woman would he recommend as a suitable wife – a woman with many cows or a maiden with flowing hair? His answer was as follows:

Between them both
I see this much and know,
I'd choose the maid
Of the combed and branching hair
By my side in bed,
Or walking thro' the fair,
Than half of Erin,
And be with a streeling wench.

The woman I'd choose myself
I will describe:
To be convivial, handsome,
Learned, fresh and kind,
Without deceit or play
Or pomp or lies:
Whate'er her fortune be,
I'd never ask or mind.

The brave yet gracious man
Who never favoured dross,
Of worldly wiles beware!
And women's favoured pass;
The herd will die,
The brindle, speckled and black.
And linked forever
To a loveless woman your lot.

PENANCE AND GRACE

As far back as I can remember we had the parish retreat. We called it mission time. It usually lasted for two weeks and was an occasion for penance always observed with great reverence and devotion. We would come home early from working in the bog, in time for attending evening sermon and devotions. One such evening we happened to meet one of the reverend fathers, who greeted us very cordially.

'Evening, boys! I suppose you have worked very hard today. Are you all coming to devotion this evening?'

We assured him that was why we had suspended work so early.

'Oh!' he said, 'excellent! Very good. Have you the turf saved for the winter fuel?'

'Yes, Father,' we said, 'it is all saved and fit for bringing home.'

'Are you all quite sure that the turf is saved?'

'Why yes, Father, we are certain.'

Then came the serious question: 'Have you your souls saved?'

We looked at one another and said in all simplicity that we did not know or we were not quite sure if our souls were saved.

The priest's countenance suddenly changed. His features now seemed grave and serious, and turning to us he said: 'I'm disappointed in you fellows. You make perfectly sure that the turf is saved, but make light of the most important harvest of all, the saving of your souls. Good evening to you, and make sure that you come to evening devotions.'

One of the boys observed that Father seemed to be getting a bit vexed. Another said perhaps he knew we were damned anyway! A third said, sure where was the use if we saved our souls that week, maybe we'd be as bad as ever the next week. However, it set us thinking about the seriousness of mortal sin and the salvation of our souls.

The mission fathers were usually of the Redemptorist Order. One would deliver mild sympathetic sermons about the love and mercy of God, while the other would thunder blood, fire and brimstone, exposing the influence of evil that we sometimes fail to notice in our lives, and the mercy of God's love which we take for granted. One evening I walked home with my neighbour, who was then an old man, after listening to a sermon on the seventh commandment. He seemed disheartened and told me about having stolen a box of boots when he was working as a deckhand among general cargo on a ship in New York harbour. After breaking open the box, he found that it contained boots which were several sizes too small for him, and on sudden impulse he dumped the box of boots into the Hudson River under cover of darkness. Several times, he said, he mentioned this in confession, only to be told by the priest in New York that he must make restitution. He said in all sincerity that he was too poor ever to be able to make restitution for a whole box of boots that had rotted in the bottom of the Hudson long years ago. I tried to tell him that God would understand how the poor are tempted to steal, but he had a different way of thinking. His argument was that poverty was a trap set for the poor, which leads them to commit sin.

The Redemptorists preached in soul-scorching terms about illicit sexual relations: the evils of the dancing hall, the dark ways home, and the frivolous parents whose failure to enforce discipline led to loose moral behaviour. Company-keeping was frowned upon in any shape or form: the only cure for illicit courting was to be salted in fasting and in penance. The girls were exhorted to forsake their lovers, and to refrain from meeting in the darkness of forbidden trysting places.

Confessions were usually heard on specially appointed days about half-way through the retreat. All the adult population availed of this opportunity. Confessions would also be heard after the evening sermon, to facilitate those who could not attend on the day appointed. A mixed queue would form outside the confessional. My teenage daughter was awaiting her turn on a certain evening. I had arranged to wait for her outside the church as it was now approaching twilight. When at last she emerged, I found she could not express herself coherently because of sudden bursts of laughter.

'Please tell me what's so funny. Did you get confession?' I asked.

'Oh yes,' she made reply, 'but something very amusing happened. When my turn came to enter the confessional, a wizened little man jumped the queue, and scooted into the box in front of me. When I walked back and took my place in the queue once more, the man standing behind me tapped on my shoulder, saying in a loud voice, "Listen girleen! Why on earth did you let that bloody bastard get ahead of you?"'

The queue shook with suppressed laughter. Even in such solemn moments, perhaps it is good for us to laugh.

Another story is told about an old couple, whom we will call Mike and Brigid. They had listened to a paint-stripping sermon on forbidden sexual relations, and were on their way homeward to their cottage under the shadow of the mountain. Mike puffed on his turned-down briar pipe, while Brigid walked beside him in pensive mood, her shawl folded across her shoulders, occasionally heaving a deep sigh. They were nearing the end of their journey when at last Brigid broke the silence.

'Mike! Did we have sexual relations?'

Mike slowly removed the pipe from his mouth and aimed a spit at the hedgerow.

'By Gemini, we did, Biddy! and not a damn one of them came to your mother's wake or funeral.'

The parish retreat usually concluded with everyone feeling better off in mind and body. The penance, the discipline, and most of all the grace of the Holy Spirit worked wonders in our lives.

I heard a wise old matron give her reasoning about large families in rural areas of Ireland and especially among the poor. We had no other form of entertainment during the long winter nights, no cinema, no dancing, nothing except going to bed with husband or wife, and the result was a large family to care for.

One of the earliest churches in the parish of Prior was a long, low, thatched house, the ruins of which were to be seen at the eastern end of Ballinskelligs beach. A little stream which runs down from Kinard East and enters the sea at this point was called The Stream of the Old Church. A tale is told of how the roof was being blown off the church one very stormy Sunday. The priest celebrating Mass became anxious and asked his congregation, 'Is there not one good man amongst you who will go out into the storm and make an effort to save your church?'

Some time elapsed before anyone made a move, as each neighbour looked at the next, waiting for the 'one good man' to arise and go out, but no one stirred, until the priest renewed his appeal to his flock. Only then did a man come forward, saying feebly: 'I am here, Father!'

The congregation burst into laughter, for this was God's fool, the man whom they said was not the full shilling, so thin and emaciated he could hide behind the handle of a garden rake. One shoulder drooped and his hair was long and unkempt. He was born thus, but he was still God's example of 'the good man'. The laughter was short-lived, as each strong man, young and old, followed God's fool out into the storm.

Times have changed. The simple faith is being challenged. Questions are being asked. Winds are blowing, some gentle, some harsh. People are looking for truth, some almost despairingly, and only death remains constant. At eighty-four years of age, sifting through accumulated beliefs, it is difficult to adjust to new formulations without having to question my own conscience, and spring-cleaning is not easy.

*   *   *

Paul and his mother came to Ballinskelligs last summer. She rented a cottage at the bend of the road, by the stream which tumbles down through the townland and into the bay. Paul had only just celebrated his seventh birthday and was his mother's only child. Each day he busied himself like a duckling in the shallow pool of the roadside stream. I asked him why he spent so much time in the stream. I got only a serious fleeting glance for an answer. It was plain that the child was building bridges with small stones and short pieces of stick.

The stream had only a couple of inches of water owing to the summer drought. Paul always wore red wellingtons. One day I sat on the bank of the stream close to where the child amused himself. He did not seem to notice my presence, and continued to build his little walls of stone. I could see that Paul was having great difficulty in constructing a bridge. Something happened every time: the stones either slipped out of place or the sticks were too short, and the walls would come tumbling down. Still, with indomitable courage, the little fellow would start all over again.

Once more I ventured to make friends with the child. Choosing my words and speaking gently, I told him in a light-hearted way that I myself was an expert in bridge-building, and boastfully claimed that I could build any kind of bridge under the sun. I

asked him if he would let me work with him at his task. After
looking at me for some time, I noticed the serious indifferent look
leave his childish features, and the light of a soft smile spread over
his face.

Together we constructed beautiful miniature bridges across the
shallow stream. With my pocket knife I cut short willow sticks
which served to span the little walls, which we then covered with
fine sandy clay. I became a friend to the child, who kept up a
constant flow of speech, some of which I didn't understand
because of the short London city accent.

That evening he took my hand and we went to meet his
mother, who thanked me for being so friendly to her son. I
promised I would come for an hour the following day to show
him how to make little boats. Next day we built a loop into the
side of the stream, representing a harbour with two headlands. I
made boats, some of paper, others of felistrim from the fronds of
the yellow iris. We used thorns of French furze for nails. When
all was finished I could see the child was delighted, and though
the little bridges were so small, in Paul's eyes and in mine they
seemed as important as Westminster, or Brooklyn Bridge. An old
neighbour who noticed us declared, 'Mike! you're reaching your
second childhood, maybe you're doting!'

I could see the sunrise of joy shining in the face of the child I
had thought to be lonely. The privilege of making friends with
Paul and watching him admire the masterpiece of his dreams
gave me a wonderful sense of satisfaction. I bade him goodbye
until tomorrow.

That night a summer thunderstorm broke over Ballinskelligs.
The clouds burst and torrents cascaded from the mountains. I
went out at about ten o'clock next morning to find the crystal
stream of the day before swollen into a frothy flood. Every trace
of the miniature harbour and bridges had been swept away,
leaving only a muddy pool. Paul stood by my side, with his hand
in mine, and I saw two tears slip slowly down his cheeks. What
had happened to his *Tír na nÓg*, his Land of Youth? I felt a lump
in my throat as I said goodbye to Paul and his mother, who were
returning to the great city. I thanked God for my friendship with

the child. For a short while it brought me back once more to my own childhood one late April when my Cremin grandmother took my hand in hers and led me across green fields to a knoll beside this same stream to pick sweet-scented bluebells and primroses.

When as a child I slept and wept –
Time crept.
When as a boy I laughed and talked –
Time walked.
When I became a full-grown man –
Time ran.
And day by day as I older grew –
Time flew.
Now I find, as I journey on –
Time gone.

SKELLIGSIDE
Southern Iveragh

IRELAND

Belfast

Sligo

Galway Dublin

Limerick

Tralee Cork

ATLANTIC OCEAN

Puff
Is.

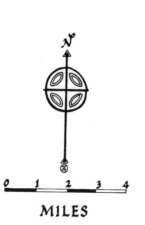

Lemon
Rock

Little
Skellig

Great
Skellig

N

0   1   2   3   4

MILES